Praise for THE OPTIMIST

"Coggins' keen observations of this genteel pursuit are offered with humor, a dash of wisdom, and an enthusiasm so infectious you'll be itching to perfect your backcast between chapters."

—*Fortune*, "Best Books of 2021"

"To paraphrase an old saying: Writing about fly fishing is like dancing about architecture. It's nearly impossible to capture, but David Coggins does it as well as anyone, and I thrilled to his adventures, from England to Patagonia to America's great rivers."

—Tom Rosenbauer, author of *The Orvis Fly-Fishing Guide*

"David Coggins is a pro, and his book is smart and aware and generous, the writing elegant, the humor tucked in just the right places."

—*TROUT Magazine*

"Anyone interested in fly fishing or curious how the sport could possibly be of interest to anyone should hop to David Coggins's excellent *The Optimist*."

—Sam Sifton, *The New York Times*

"Lively, humoristic but informative . . . [Coggins is] a talented and entertaining writer."

—*Atlantic Salmon Journal*

"[*The Optimist*] makes a nice philosophical case for fly fishing."

—*GQ*

"I've fished many of the rivers in this book, but I hadn't seen them run and shimmer the way they do in Coggins's lively prose. What's more, I'd given up on fishing, I don't know why—maybe I've been preoccupied with ephemera rather than the eternal, which is what fly fishing makes one confront. I closed the last chapter and said, hell or high water, I was going to get back to the rivers and streams I've missed. There's much to fall in love with in this world, and this book reminded me of that."
—Doug Stanton, #1 *New York Times* bestselling author
of *Horse Soldiers*

"Humorous and relatable . . . A great read for fly fishing enthusiasts and novices alike."
—*Flylords*

"*The Optimist* is a rueful, thoughtful, and very funny examination of an elegant obsession. Coggins does a terrific job of evoking the joys of fly fishing and also the frustrations, which are inextricably linked. This is the best book I've read on fishing since Thomas McGuane's *The Longest Silence*."
—Jay McInerney, author of *A Hedonist in the Cellar*
and *Bright, Precious Days*

"Wonderfully written, consistently amusing, grand but never grandiose."
—Lesley M. M. Blume, author of *Fallout*

"An excellent primer for the beginning fly angler and a lyrical reminder of all there is to love about the sport for even the most jaded of old hands."
—Monte Burke, author of *Lords of the Fly* and *Saban*

"A modern fly fishing classic."
—*Oppstrøms* magazine (Norway)

"A pure and extended love letter to fishing . . . What grows on you and ultimately stays with you while reading *The Optimist* is his sheer exuberance and honesty. The real brotherhood of fishing might occasionally be about fishing triumphs, but just as often if not more, it is about failures. And we get streamside seats to all of Coggins's."

—*The Washington Free Beacon*

"A wise, affectionate chronicle of a passion pursued."

—*Kirkus Reviews*

"The personal is what makes *The Optimist* such a welcome addition to the part of your bookshelf dedicated to hobbies and sport."

—*InsideHook*

"A lovely, ruminative book about a venerable sport . . . Coggins's enthusiasm for fly fishing is so infectious that the book will readily hook non-fishers as well."

—*Library Journal*

Also by David Coggins

Men and Style

Men and Manners

THE
OPTIMIST

A CASE FOR THE FLY FISHING LIFE

DAVID COGGINS

SCRIBNER

New York   London   Toronto   Sydney   New Delhi

Scribner
An Imprint of Simon & Schuster, Inc.
1230 Avenue of the Americas
New York, NY 10020

First Scribner trade paperback edition May 2022

SCRIBNER and design are registered trademarks of The Gale Group, Inc.,
used under license by Simon & Schuster, Inc., the publisher of this work.

For information about special discounts for bulk purchases,
please contact Simon & Schuster Special Sales at 1-866-506-1949
or business@simonandschuster.com.

The Simon & Schuster Speakers Bureau can bring authors to your live event. For
more information, or to book an event, contact the Simon & Schuster Speakers
Bureau at 1-866-248-3049 or visit our website at www.simonspeakers.com.

Interior design by Erich Hobbing

1 3 5 7 9 10 8 6 4 2

Library of Congress Cataloging-in-Publication Data has been applied for.

ISBN 978-1-9821-5250-5
ISBN 978-1-9821-5251-2 (pbk)
ISBN 978-1-9821-5252-9 (ebook)

CONTENTS

CONTENTS

THE OPTIMIST

THE CONTRARY ACT

INTRODUCTION

Moving water thrills me. I can't drive over a bridge without looking down at the river and wondering whether trout live there. I speculate about where they might be hiding and how I'd try to catch them. Then I break from my reverie before I swerve into oncoming traffic. If I've decided the river's promising, I privately plot a return. It's like discovering a secret hidden in plain sight.

The discovery is bittersweet, however, because the chances of coming back are low. Life interferes with the best angling intentions. I've studied maps with snaking blue lines and evocative names waiting to be fished: the Jefferson, the Test, the Spey, the Alta. There's so much water, and it takes years, longer, to learn a river's nature. The names of rivers I've yet to fish are etched in my head like the titles of great novels sitting unread on the shelf. I'm still trying to understand the rivers in my life beyond the most basic familiarity. Beneath the surface are mysteries we can barely make out, so we study and speculate and remember every detail we can. This is fishing.

By fishing, I mean fly fishing, with its traditional way of casting, wading or from a drift boat, often for trout. But also salmon, bonefish, striped bass, and more, all over the world. The obsession, when it takes hold, is global and total. A friend has an insight—*Everybody knows about the salmon fishing in Iceland, but did you hear about their brown trout?*—apparently it's great, and I find myself on an esoteric website at midnight in a language I don't read.

Angling is about anticipation and planning trips far in the future, but it also has a storied history. This sport has been practiced since Izaak Walton's *Compleat Angler* was published in 1653, in ways that are, to the naked eye, fairly unchanged today, like a Shakespeare play performed on a thrust stage. Some people justify fly fishing with claims that it's poetic, and, yes, there are moments of pure poetry, but the pleasures of fishing are also tactile and immediate. The theoretical considerations tend to enter my mind, sometimes against my will, when I'm not catching anything.

THE CONTRARY ACT

When upstanding yet angling-agnostic citizens find out I'm fishing for a week in Montana, they raise an eyebrow; when they find out I'm going to the Bahamas, they raise two. It's as if I'm not merely leaving town but leaving society, the society that's employed, productive, efficient, and to their mind, necessary. Fishing in the modern world, I've come to realize, is a contrary act. While it might improve one's moral character (a possibly dubious theory), to fish with purpose and intensity, to seek sporting opportunities in far-flung places, strikes many as decadent.

Perhaps fishing is decadent, but it didn't always seem that way. I began fishing as a boy not because I thought it was morally redeeming, but because I loved it. If anything, it felt natural. We had a cabin on a lake in Wisconsin, and what could make more sense than to row a boat out into the bay and cast to bass as the sun went down over the trees? What I enjoyed then I still enjoy now: the solitude and mystery, the bursts of action, the near misses, the occasional triumphs and, when it's over, rowing home in silence, the water smooth as glass.

As a man, standing in a stream on a weekday afternoon in late spring, casting to trout, is a more conscious decision. I still do it for the sheer joy of being outside, of concentrating, of the doubts and rewards of being connected to a fish, of landing and releasing it. Fishing offers an internal reward, and that personal satisfaction is enough. This is the same reason why a good lunch—a proper three-hour lunch, where wine is ordered by the bottle not the glass—is so rare and rewarding. This escape is not exactly illicit, but it certainly takes you outside the course of events of the day.

Fishing is waiting. When I'm on the water, I'm out of time and the world recedes. Even when nothing seems to be happening, *something* is happening. The seeming nothing is what gives shape to the eruption of activity, it offers a symmetry, though really an asymmetry, to the strike. Tom McGuane wrote that it's the long stretches of silence that give fishing its purpose. When Countess Almaviva sings her aria at the end of *The Marriage of Figaro*, it's one of the most beautiful passages in music. You can listen to it anytime, but if you watch the opera at the Met it's four hours into the production. Getting to that point reveals the burden of her character's loss and the delicate forgiveness of her husband. All that time is necessary to feel the full weight of what she's singing. Similarly, catching a fish without waiting is a distorted experience. You can't live on dessert alone.

And yet even waiting on the water I'm more engaged than I am anywhere else. An angler is sensitive to changes in the weather, to shade and sun, to any movement on the stream. There are clues everywhere lightly hidden: which insects are appearing that a trout might eat, the speed of the current, shadows faintly moving under the water. When this knowledge converges with enough skill and conspires with luck, I might catch a fish.

But more often I don't catch a fish. That's why fishing requires coming to terms with the fact that you can do everything exactly the way you want to and still fail. Are you comfortable with that? I hope so. Fishing measures success in an invisible way. Most fly fishing is catch and release, by rule or by principle. At the end of the day, there's nothing to show for it. Catching a fish first exists in the moment and then in the memory, like childhood, with photos that don't do the experience justice.

When people ask me about the attraction to fishing, which they often do because they genuinely want to know or are mildly exasperated that I do it, I tell them that it's an outdoor sport. This is obvious of course, but it's the basic truth. You're in the natural world, usually in a beautiful place. I read once that if you stand all day on a typical east-west street in Manhattan, like the one I live on, you'll receive eight minutes of direct sunlight. I don't know if that's true, but it certainly *feels* true. When I go fishing, I know I'll be outside for the next eight hours with as much direct sunlight as I want.

There are the angling specifics, the rituals and peripheral pleasures that are also part of the sport. Early breakfast at a saloon before driving into Yellowstone National Park, hash browns well done. Buying ice at the gas station, picking up lunch. Talking to the slightly dismissive men at the local fly shop and trying to sort out their cryptic advice about what's been working. They possess the superior air of harboring secret knowledge that record store clerks used to have. The curious glances at the trucks driven by guides hauling drift boats—and guides always drive trucks, usually with a crack snaking across the windshield.

There are codes which exist in any intense pursuit. There are outright snobs, reverse snobs, and people so isolated they can't be considered either. There are those who embrace the new, wear highly technical clothes and endorse the latest technology. There are anglers who are so passionately behind the times they wear waxed canvas, which is heavy, hot, and doesn't even keep the water out when it really needs to; they do this as a point of tradition and pride. There are the bamboo anglers who track down and then spend a small fortune for a rod made by one specific builder who's usually dead. The bamboo rod becomes like a suit of clothes that's so nice you can't wear it—the rod is too valuable to actually fish with. Yes, members of these irrational subgenres are part of the angling world as well. Sometimes, in polite society, we recognize one another.

That's why anglers are like spies. We keep our motives to ourselves, the details and schemes can't be shared with anybody who's not a fellow traveler in this world of secret obsession. Some of this is social convenience, to keep from boring civilians who are disinterested, incredulous, or downright opposed. In my family of angling agnostics, there's a highly enforced one-minute rule on fishing stories. Anything longer leads to relatives with unfocused eyes settling in the middle distance. I admit my fishing desire can be so intense I don't like to describe it to the unafflicted. I don't want other people to know, and perhaps I don't want to admit to myself, just how much I think about fishing. There's something slightly suspicious about this devotion, like a weakness for absinthe, an eccentric habit that should be tempered before it turns into a depraved addiction. Too much fishing—and too much absinthe for that matter—can leave you with an overgrown beard, far from home, raving about the fate of the world. It's like I'm part of a disreputable cult known to have suspect views about the creation of the universe. But now I'm a true believer.

THE CONTRARY ACT

• • •

There's a spring creek not far from Livingston. It's late summer. I pull off the paved road and drive slowly through fields, waiting for the cows to move out of the way. I park and open a beer. This is in Montana, and you can't buy beer in a grocery store on Sundays before 9 a.m., which is a lesson you only need to learn once, and now I buy it the night before.

This time of preparation—assembling the rod, pulling on waders, lacing up boots, tying on flies—is one of my favorite parts of fishing. Angling is more than being on the water—it's the entire day, the anticipation, the fishing of course, the stories afterward, the remembering and then the misremembering. The same way that going to lunch at Le Grand Véfour means walking through the Palais Royal and wondering what you're going to order. I take my time; the angling day is still full of possibility, and I can't help envisioning potential triumphs while ignoring the more likely small, morale-fraying setbacks that are intrinsic to the sport.

One thing that always surprises me whenever I arrive at streams is how harmless they feel, innocent of my intentions. Tall grasses and low willow trees blow sleepily along the bank. It's just another day, with only slight variations of countless other days here. What's different is that on this day I'm here, I want to intersect with everything that's unfolding on its own. The seeming sense of peace on the water gives way, under observation, to furious activity that's nearly invisible to those not attuned to it.

Looking closely reveals signs of life, trout coming up and feeding near the surface. Tactically, that means fishing a dry fly—one that floats—which remains the platonic ideal of the sport. If all goes well, you see the fish break the water and take your fly, an eternal thrill. This makes me excited and a little nervous, now I have to make decisions. The fish are doing their part, I have to do mine. I choose a Royal Trude, rust and white, and then tie on something to a line behind it, a smaller dry fly, a little blue-winged olive, the size of a used pencil eraser, to float a few feet after it. Presumably this gives me more chances, or at least allows me the illusion that I'm being scientific.

My first cast is a bad cast. It's too short and not even straight. This is a tradition of mine. I don't start well. Have you met somebody you find attractive and made a witty remark to them right out of the gate? Well then congratulations, perhaps you of iron nerves and sharp presence of mind can come catch this trout. I, however, need to warm up.

The drift is the goal. The drift is everything. When the fly floats seamlessly in the current over a feeding fish, the anticipation is real. I'm waiting, praying, it will come up and take the fly. These moments when the fly passes above the head of a trout are wonderful and excruciating. This is the same rush of excitement gamblers feel when they scratch off a lottery ticket. They don't really think they're going to win—they know better—it's the chance of winning they're addicted to. That's the same when you fish. The possibility keeps you making one more cast.

During the drift, one second, two, three, an interminable four seconds, anything is possible. Then suddenly it's not at all possible. The fly was rejected, ignored. Was it the drift, was it the fly? The fish are still out there, they're still feeding. But not on my Royal Trude, not on my blue-winged olive. The water is clear—they definitely saw it. They just didn't like it. I take stock, get technical and tie on an emerger pattern. This imitates an insect evolving from a larva to an adult; it sits in the film of water and is harder to see. I take my time, which is difficult when the fish are feeding right in front of me.

I make the cast where I want to, a small triumph, and the fly floats over the trout's head. Or at least where it was a few seconds ago. Then: a minor hiccup in the surface, like a small pebble fell into the water. The trout. No matter how many times this happens the action still feels abrupt. The fish took the fly, but until I raise my rod it's impossible to know if the trout's hooked. When the line tightens and I feel the pressure, that steady weight, a sideways movement of its head, only then do I know for sure. That's the vital moment. The fish is on.

This state of affairs seems to extend endlessly—though it's only about a second—then the trout heads away from me—and quickly. I want to see that fish, I want to know what I'm dealing with. So many things can go wrong if it jumps from the water, it might throw out the hook. But it can also break the fine line if I pull it too insistently. If it swims too far downstream it might keep going and break off that way. I know all this because I've lost fish almost every way imaginable, especially on this stream, and they all hurt differently. All happy fish stories are alike. Each unhappy one is unhappy in its own way.

With steady pressure on the line I finally bring the fish near the bank. I raise the rod even farther and slide the fish over my net. This is also delicate, because a trout usually makes one last dash, and when it's this close, it's a very unpleasant time to come up short. But this time it works. It all works. The fish is lovely, a long, healthy cutthroat trout, gold and deep pink, its eye black and unblinking in the shallow water. I don't need a photo. I revive it, and once it feels like itself it swims back down to the bottom of the pool.

The drama's over in two minutes, maybe three. When everything succeeds, it seems inevitable, even easy in a way. How else was it supposed to happen? Well, there are so many ways to be heartbroken on the water that sometimes the joy comes from merely avoiding mistakes or bad luck. Catching a fish brings the simple satisfaction and absolute fact of everything unfolding as planned. The presentation of a fly, managing the drift, the physical action of fighting a fish and successfully landing it. This never feels like I'm taming nature, more like being in alignment, and understanding it better, at least for a short time. Fishing is a search for the fleeting connection to something alive that can never be fully known. Once the fish is gone, it's just me on the bank. There are mountains in the distance. Nobody knows where I am. Sometimes you get lucky.

This book is about the pursuit of fishing. That pursuit means learning specific angling skills—casting, managing line, selecting flies, fighting fish. It also means refining more universal virtues: patience, careful observation, self-containment. Angling doesn't exist in a vacuum, it unfolds in spectacular locations all over the world. This book visits places with their own traditions beyond angling, from grilled *asada* dinners next to the great rivers of Patagonia, to landing a float plane in remote ponds in northern Maine. There are the dramatic landscapes, from the mountain streams of Montana to the isolated flats of the Bahamas.

Fishing requires skill and experience, but it also requires an act of faith. By definition we control only part of the equation. The fish has to complete the loop. That means living with the knowledge that success, as it's traditionally defined, requires something out of your control. That's why an angler must, at some level, be an optimist. There's no other way to cast and cast with long odds and no possibility of reward. Of course, casting in a beautiful setting can be its own reward, but sometimes there needs to be a trout at the end of the line. And while every angler has his faith tested, the true ones return to the water because they believe. That belief is one of the themes of this book.

The Optimist traces my angling education and recounts my progression from apprentice to obsessive. There's something rational about angling—a precise progression of logical tactics. But there's also something slightly unhinged about it. My desire can't really be contained, it flows like water into every corner of my life, and now I can't stop thinking about trout. Angling threatens to take me away from the responsibilities of life. *Are you going fishing?* a loved one asks, her slightly judgmental tone seems to linger in the air. *Yes, I told you the other day*, I answer sheepishly. *I mentioned it briefly when you were distracted* (I fail to add). And that's a strange part of its appeal. It's easy to get addicted to living among anglers in a world that's parallel to the more responsible one most people inhabit.

I'm not alone. The world is full of angling eccentrics, from Bahamian lodge owners to Low Country guides, Colorado boat builders to Catskills fly tiers. Within the world of fly fishing there are obsessives at another level beyond me who have devoted their lives to the pursuit even if that means, *especially* if that means, leading unorthodox lives. Not just hobbyists who build rods or tie flies, but men and women who guide half the year in Wyoming and then go to Chile to guide another five months (keeping a month for their own fishing in between).

The Optimist makes the case for ideals beyond angling, for a set of skills that are practiced, improved upon, and measured over time. Taken together they lead to a stronger connection to the natural world and to the enduring belief that something good might happen on that next cast and if not then certainly the one after that. Anglers might be ornery and they might still tell stories about a fish they lost decades ago — *You should have seen it*, they whisper as the fire dies out, *I swear to you*, swear to you, *it was thirty inches* — but, in the end, every committed angler is an optimist. There's no other way. If there's one thing I love about talking to anglers it's this gleam in their eye, they can't hide the childlike fact that they still believe.

This is a book about the specifics of angling and what it takes to do it well. But it's also about the world that opens up as you master those skills. Fishing has taken me worldwide. I've met devotees in a small Belize airport, in a makeshift bar known to anglers who pose for photos with the ancient bartender. I've met them in a diner on a desolate Canadian highway on the way to go salmon fishing. Stories are exchanged with knowing glances. This book is about the passion and irrationality that leads to those connections.

A good angler has an attitude that reflects a worldview, even a sense of style that communicates a personality. A lucky hat, a few dubious theories, some secret knowledge, an invented fly, a hidden flask, a sense of the improbable. They've learned things over time: the best cigar store in Buenos Aires, which rum to buy in Nassau, a trusted bush pilot in Alaska. These are the hallmarks of the obsessed. It's a club that's open to anybody dedicated to one of the world's enduring sports.

Are you a believer? Good. Welcome to the game.

WISCONSIN

SMALLMOUTH BASS

Timing

Since fly fishing is learned, it requires a teacher. That's why all anglers have mentors, whether an obsessed neighbor, an uncle held in disrepute, or a father intent on handing down his passion, whether the next generation is willing or not. The men who taught me to fish were friends of my grandfather's, legendary figures on the lake in Wisconsin where we all had cabins. Their angling inheritance had reached the end of their own family lines, and there I was. At twenty, I was older than a teenager who could be a true disciple, properly schooled. In theory, I should have been better sooner, but neither Dave nor Carter was picky. They'd arrived at the point when they needed somebody, anybody, to go out on day trips to rivers with them. I'd like to think my personality was part of the appeal. It wasn't.

Carter and Dave were each looking for an accomplice who could drive a car, paddle a canoe, and, crucially, not talk too much. Fishing from a boat involves a great deal of sitting in silence. With older men, I've learned, when in doubt speak less. I kept quiet and tried to learn. All anglers have their own styles and idiosyncrasies, and I was lucky to receive my angling education from two men with very different attitudes. One man represented reason, the other emotion.

The first was Carter, a tactician and a rationalist. For him, fishing was a science that required firsthand knowledge and a series of viable, never desperate, alternatives. Catching a fish involved clear parameters and internal logic that meant changing flies regularly depending upon success, or lack of it. We might not solve these fish, he advocated, but we would understand them better.

In my memory Carter was tall and well built, though that may have been because all adults seem large to younger people. Like many anglers, he was rarely seen without a hat. Thick glasses made his eyes look large, and you felt under scrutiny when you tried to do something that he could have done at a much more advanced level. All of that made him intimidating to me, though I later realized just how patient he was with my learning curve.

Carter brought clarity to a mysterious process. The only other option was chaos, which was close at hand but unacceptable. We would observe our surroundings, recognize what we knew to be true and should be true, and, in the end, we should triumph. If we did not carry the day, then it was because the universe had conspired to undermine us. We had done all we could and, as a result, could bear no blame.

My other mentor was Dave. He did none of this. Dave was a willful man so far beyond stubborn that the word lost its meaning. He tried to overtake cars in the passing lane when he had no earthly reason to think he could. The car in front of us may indeed have been going too slow, but we could not necessarily go faster, because we were in a Ford Astro van Dave had retrofitted by removing the way back seat, creating enough space for an electric motorbike or a dead deer. These passing expeditions often took place while we were pulling a boat on a trailer, mind you, out of principle and impatience, and lasted a knuckle-whitening ten seconds, while oncoming traffic on Wisconsin country roads grew increasingly larger. We passed successfully through Dave's will alone.

Dave reminded me of a bear. He had high shoulders perfectly built for carrying a canoe over his head, and he walked with a slight limp (he was always getting into scrapes and laughing about them later). This intensity of purpose carried into Dave's fishing. He decided how he wanted to fish a situation and would not change, hour after hour, day after day. Eventually, all these days turned into years. Why would you alter what's already irrefutable, even when results imply otherwise? Dave had retired from trout fishing in Montana (which he said had gotten too crowded) and then trout fishing in Northern Wisconsin (the water had gotten too warm and damaged the fishing). He fished in Florida in the winter. But this was summer, and we pursued smallmouth bass out of a canoe in small rivers, with poppers cast to the bank. All. Day. Long. The clarity of intent and sheer willfulness in Dave's approach was admirable and, at times, maddening.

Dave and Carter knew each other well, and fished together for decades, but that was in the past by the time either one invited me to fish with him. Carter suffered from various ailments, some of which Dave thought were in his imagination, and he struggled fishing out of a canoe (Dave's preferred mode). There's an old story on our lake that once they ran into each other in the dark on a river famous for a late-night mayfly hatch. People would drive for hours to fish this water as it approached midnight. The black sky was full of a blizzard of insects, like a nocturnal snowstorm. When the mayflies settled on the water, large trout would rise and take them aggressively. On a moonless night you couldn't see the fish, only hear them.

It's hard to believe Dave and Carter could make each other out in the dark but they did. It was a place so secret they had kept it from one another. I gather it was rather awkward. But they recognized something in each other, a shared deep local knowledge and then a propensity for secrecy, even among friends, which they respected as part of the angler's creed.

Each would make slightly provocative remarks about the other's habits in his absence. "Carter is always *fiddling* around in his tackle box," Dave would say, with the emphasis on "fiddling" which implied a needless, even feckless, lack of belief. This sort of fiddling, if left unchecked, upset classical trains of thought; it was the type of thinking that led to New Coke.

Carter was intrigued by "David's fancy bass boat," so carefully designed and built it could move in only six inches of water, which he considered decadent, when a basic jon boat would do just fine. Carter called him David—he was one of few to do so, and I interpreted that as a sign of their closeness. Carter said, "David doesn't change and will *never* change." I couldn't tell if he meant Dave's personality or his fishing tactics, not that Carter, or Dave for that matter, made a distinction between the two.

Dave and Carter both loved smallmouth bass, and their love converted me. A smallmouth bass is a strong game fish, not elegant and streamlined like the trout (which I preferred, I realize now, because of its not insignificant provenance). As Dave often said when trying to land a particularly strong-willed bass, "It thinks it's bigger than it is."

The smallmouth bass lives in warm water and is not snobby. Where we fished, they were brown with wide black stripes, a large one, fattened on crayfish, resembled a flattened football. The trout prefers cold water and cares about its reputation, like an English aristocrat. It's usually brilliantly colored with vivid spots. The smallmouth is strong and will fight, and when you catch one it pulls and pulls. Finally, you reel it in, grab it by the mouth and unhook it and it will swim right away without resentment. Trout are more delicate, more discerning, more distinguished. Trout hold grudges.

The first time I went on a trip with Dave, more than twenty years ago now, was to a river an hour and a half north of the lake where we lived each summer. I was to arrive at his house at 8 a.m. Instructions were simple: Bring lunch and a rod. I would take our ancient motorboat over to his cabin, which was a more direct (and more poetic) way than driving around the dirt roads that added miles to the trip.

I was not my most efficient that morning and arrived at 8:10 a.m. Dave didn't comment on my lateness and didn't have to. He was sitting in his van with the engine running. His greeting was only "You can put your lunch in the cooler," and that was it until we got on the highway about ten minutes later. It felt much longer than that. I was never late again, except when the temperamental motor on our boat died and I had to row the rest of the way across the lake. Dave was prepared and saw me approach through his binoculars, though not before calling our house and waking my father at an ungodly hour. Of course, Dave didn't believe in ungodly hours if fishing was involved, but, like a lot of old-timers, he woke up at five anyway.

We rumbled down curved country roads with a canoe strapped to the roof of the van, past dairy farms with old barns and black-and-white cows who slowly turned their heads toward us before resuming their grassy meal. If we saw prosperous fields of green soybeans or healthy corn, Dave might say, "Now, that looks like a pretty squared away operation." Carter and Dave both spoke in a way that reminded me, correctly or not, of the 1950s. So did my late grandfather, who always pronounced airplane as "aero-plane" as if he were still thrilled by this miraculous new invention. A law professor at the University of Chicago, Walter was less interested in farming than politics, architecture, and art, though he too loved this part of the country. Every year my grandparents would go on canoe trips with Dave, Carter, and their wives. Naturally, Dave planned the whole thing.

Dave turned north, and we left the flat country and drove up into the hills, which were not too high, but high enough to look down into the mellow fields below, which had the reassuring green geometry of Dutch landscape paintings. We moved onto quieter roads, and Dave asked me questions about where I lived in Manhattan, and was scandalized when I told him the cost of a monthly parking place (not that I had one in any case). After ninety minutes we pulled up to a bridge with water running under it. I was instructed never to reveal the name of this river to anybody, especially "any of my friends from the city," whom he invoked in ominous tones. He was worried they might head to this remote area with their Range Rovers, hypoallergenic dogs, and YETI coolers full of orange wine. I didn't mention the name then and won't mention it now, in honor of Dave, and the enduring principle of never revealing another angler's discovery.

A moment after we arrived, another car pulled nearby. This surprised me, but Dave just said, "That's Lorne," and walked over. I was intrigued. On the drive up Lorne had not been mentioned, but clearly he was part of some intricate plan. We had driven an hour and a half, stopped for gas, made up the ten minutes due to my tardiness, and then met Lorne, who lived nearby, within moments of our arrival. This operation had the efficiency of a bank heist.

Lorne would be our shuttle. Anybody who floats down a river needs their van or truck waiting for them down at the takeout. In a remote area there's no clever way to do this, though that didn't keep us from trying schemes that involved bicycling on the highway. Essentially, somebody drives down with you, waits while you park, then drives you back, in their car, to where you'll put your boat in. Then you pay them. This service is about the purest form of capitalism there is.

In certain places out West, where a lot of people take float trips, it's been raised to an art form. Well, if not an art form then at least a streamlined operation, a two-man job: A guide calls an outfitter and says, "My truck is up here, please drop it down there." Generally, they hide the keys in the gas cap or under the mat in the driver's seat. If you stop in a parking lot at a popular fishing spot in Montana and see a truck with an empty boat trailer behind it, you can probably find the keys rather easily. It's not unknown to be fishing and halfway through the day the guide will look up and wave to the shuttle hauling his truck down the highway.

Certain men from the country spend their whole lives outside and seem reflexively drawn to the shade. They wear hats and tinted glasses, their stubble's haphazard, it's hard to get a good look at them. If they arrive at an event with their hair combed back, in their best shirt, you might not even recognize them. That was Lorne. He was old enough that you didn't ask how old he was. He had one pair of jeans, held up with suspenders, which seemed to get larger every year. Later, at the beginning of each summer, I would ask Dave if Lorne was (dramatic pause) doing well. Dave knew I wanted to know if Lorne was still alive. He would laugh and say, "Yeah, Lorne made it through another winter." He was as surprised as I was.

A woman sat in the passenger seat, Jeanine. It wasn't clear what the arrangement was between them; she was much younger and quite pretty. In later years she would drive and Lorne was the passenger. We took off the canoe and our cooler, the dry bag, and Dave's beloved tackle box. I assembled our rods and packed the boat and waited while they drove five or six miles downriver to the takeout to leave Dave's van. Then they brought Dave back upriver and we gave them $20, which presumably was a fair amount of Lorne's income.

You have to imagine that everything Dave says has an exclamation point after it. He spent most of his life outside and had no indoor voice. When he had a fish on, he would speak even louder and keep telling his story uninterrupted. And he was usually the one telling the story. He was still excited even after all these years and all these fish. On very rare occasions, when he considered that he had made a mistake that cost him a good fish, he would pause, let the situation sink in, then howl, "Shit!" It was like a thunderclap. He still cared.

Most of our fishing was on small rivers, out of a canoe. We would float between willow trees and banks of wild rice, still green in summer, an eagle circling suspiciously overhead as we got closer to its nest, Joe Pye weed, in pink bloom, grew on the marshy islands that divided the channels. If you were observing us from a distance, it would look like a very slow canoe trip. But of course it was not merely a canoe trip. We had further motives.

Now, as everyone knows, the cast is the basic unit of angling. It's been written about, fretted over, and parsed with the intensity of a rediscovered Renaissance masterpiece. There are so many truisms to casting it's easy to wonder which are actually true. For such an analyzed act the motion of a cast is very concise.

In your hand is a fly rod (so you've already made a good decision about your day). The reel holds a fly line, which floats and is usually a discreet shade of green and sometimes an upsetting bright orange. Attached to the end of the fly line is a thin, translucent leader, which gets narrower at its end and transforms into tippet material, which looks as fine as a strand in a spider's web. This tippet is tied to the fly itself. The goal is for the fly to land delicately on the water with a minimum of disturbance. Casting a fly rod looks easy but, unfortunately, it is not.

When you're fishing with conventional tackle (a spinning reel), the weight of the lure will carry the cast out a great distance. Fly anglers shun such ease, out of principle, a sense of sport, or a dash of snobbism, and usually all three. Instead, the movement of the fly rod back and forth increases the speed of the line until there's enough momen-

ads in a great unfurl-

y twenty, thirty, forty

sure if this sounds easy

when somebody is good,

made it look effortless. So

s this effortlessness that gets

Je. Casting is not something that

y by moving your arm faster, it can

iming. And mastering this timing, alas,

y personal casting recipe (adjust to taste):

Point your rod straight ahead. Pull as much line extended in front of you into the water as you want to cast.
- Raise your forearm quickly. Lift your hand to your ear, as if you were answering a phone.
- Wait while the fly line extends behind you. This is the back cast, the less romantic but crucial sibling to the more theatrical forward cast.
- When the line is extended all the way behind you, about, but not quite, a second later, quickly cast forward again, concisely as if you were flicking a dart, not a long motion as if you were throwing a football (which is what most people do, using strength of arm to make up for the line speed that comes with good timing).
- In a perfect world, the cast unfurls in what's called a loop. The fly delicately lands on the water and you feel like a goddamn genius.

This act was described memorably in
Through It by Norman Maclean (who knew
ther when they both taught at the University
Now, Norman's father, the minister, describes
"an art that is performed on a four-count rhythm
ten and two o'clock." This passage is so famous it p
to be contrary—though contrary is what most angler
help being since we are serial correctors, refiners, in
theorists, and provocateurs. I have to note that in my ex
rience the 10 to 2 motion of the rod is more like 9 to 1.
fact, just reviewing the opening pages of the book, the min
ister reveals that it's really closer to 1 than to 2, which, since
we're now in closer agreement, is very reassuring.

To cast forward a long way you first must cast backward a long way (that would be the back cast). So on long casts Dave would have to let more line travel behind him, and the fly would travel, hook and all, at high speed directly over my head in the back of the canoe. His timing was so good that he could increase the distance of his casts and intuitively let the back cast wait one fraction of a second longer to extend completely. He would complete his forward cast, and somehow, miraculously, the popper would travel through the air right where he wanted it to go, every time.

Sometimes I would lose the vital sense of timing and my back casts would end up slapping the water behind us. I've caught weeds, trees, and people with my back casts. Sometimes on three consecutive casts, a trifecta of ignominy, leaving me swearing under my breath and sometimes not under it. Once the timing of the cast deserts you, then it takes a moment or two to get it back. This can happen because your arm is tired, because you're tense trying to make a good cast to a promising stretch of water, or just because the angling gods are testing you. And they will test you.

On the river that day I fished first—and, as I was painfully aware, and Dave would soon see, I hadn't done much fishing from a canoe before. The whole business of casting is complicated when you're in a canoe. Casting seated is harder than casting standing up, but standing would tip the boat. A fly rod is not designed to be cast this way—my back cast would be flying over Dave's head. Which meant the fly, with a hook the size of a thumb, would head directly at Dave and hopefully above him. I promptly caught Dave's hat, on my second cast. "It's not the first time I've been hooked," he said, surprisingly unbothered. Then he added, in case I was about to get too comfortable with such amateur maneuvers, "But I don't always like it."

Our goal was to cast as closely as we could to the bank, let the fly rest for a second, give it a pop or two, and if we were lucky a bass would come from its hiding place—its lie—creating a wake of water, and devour the fly in a spectacular turn. Imagine a submerged beach ball bursting through the top of a river. These dramatic takes are part of the thrill of bass fishing on the surface, a disruption of a summer calm.

We fished with poppers. A trout fly is a delicate, airy combination of feathers and fur that is an intricate construction worthy of a trout, which has high self-esteem. A popper is nothing like that. It looks like half a wine cork painted green or yellow or black, with little squiggly plastic legs. There are photography books devoted to trout and salmon flies. There are no books with artfully lit poppers. They're usually made of foam, some still use painted cork that chips after catching many fish, and some anglers continue to use half-destroyed poppers, with scars of past bass battles. Poppers float easily, and when pulled across the water they dart, making the popping sound they're named for. To the fish they might resemble a frog, nobody really knows for sure. Anglers have their preferred color based on how clear the water is, how bright the day, or some personal experience or superstition. I liked black, though I briefly had a yellow phase. Dave stuck with green.

In those days while I was still learning, Dave would give me suggestions about where to cast. These were delivered with a surprisingly diplomatic touch: "You might want to try on the other bank, where the current picks up." He was looking farther down the river than I was. Over the years I began to anticipate where to cast, and his suggestions became quite rare. The bass liked the current since the current brought food. They didn't like stagnant water—pike and muskies liked that, but we only caught them by accident, and their sharp teeth would break our leaders and send the poppers off down river, Dave hurrying to gather them to save a two-dollar fly.

Once I learned what was at stake, I realized how much more I had to learn. That's often the case in angling, as in anything worthwhile. The difference between an average cast and a good cast is about six inches. Beyond good is expert, and that's the territory Dave inhabited. Dave devoted his life to sport and fished a hundred days a year for sixty years of his life. Sometimes more. He also hunted grouse, geese, ducks, turkeys. He was an outstanding angler and could cast his popper within an inch or two of the bank, which is exactly what you want to do. You couldn't swim over there and place it down any better than that. He could do it into the wind in a moving canoe I was struggling to control as the current picked up. It's an almost secret skill that matters only to those who've tried to do it enough to know how hard it is. And the skill, which is true of everything in casting, involves timing.

I rarely commented to Dave about his extraordinary casting. I preferred to marvel privately. When we began fishing together, I couldn't get my casts right to the bank. I told myself I was close enough. In a lot of fishing, however, a few inches is exactly what does matter. After we'd been fishing for a few years, Dave told me I'd improved. This was out of character for him and exciting for me even though it was delivered at the expense of my earlier self, who now somewhat embarrassed me. Just how bad had I been?

Only when I'd fished with him for years did I have the confidence to say to Dave, "That was well done," when he had made a particularly difficult cast under an overhanging tree. Normally we didn't compliment each other, but we might use a code, usually after a good cast to a promising place with no results. When I had evolved into a better caster, he might say, "You can't do any more than that." This wasn't meant to placate, just to acknowledge that we'd done what we set out to do. Though Dave might have the last word. After a particularly long drought, he would explode: "Ornery critters!"

Nearly every meaningful thing I've ever learned was only clear in retrospect. What I learned from Dave were countless incidental tactics. How to maneuver a popper delicately around a tree lying in the river. How to cast sidearm under branches, an unorthodox faster motion than an overhead cast. It required a good sense of timing because the fly line was traveling backward, close to the water, and you didn't want it to fall in.

Gradually I realized that I didn't have to think about the timing as much. It started to come naturally to me, and I would wait a split second longer when I was trying to cast a greater distance. Mastering casting's sense of timing happens through repetition—the body has to internalize it, the mind can't just enforce it. Ultimately, the rod feels less like a tool than a part of you. I realize that this is one of the first things you're taught when learning to fish—"let the rod be an extension of your arm"—but it took me years to really understand what that meant. When I did, the rod finally started bending to my will.

Other things that looked easy when Dave did them were impossible for me to do when I tried. He could keep a canoe still in the current holding one oar and moving it around in a circle, like he was stirring a large cocktail. I've never been able to master it. He didn't formally explain things to me, I just imitated what he did. Eventually I was able to get my casts where I wanted them. I could never catch all the way up. He still saw everything before I did. There was not a deer or an osprey that he didn't see first, despite the fact he was forty years my senior.

And he could, crucially, see fish very well. Bass will take a popper dramatically in a flash of water. But sometimes the popper simply disappears with barely a ripple, in what Dave would call a "little sippy take." You'd better be paying attention or you'd miss it and not set the hook in time. Plenty of big fish take flies very delicately, so don't think a quiet take means a small fish.

I would ask Dave how he found the rivers where we fished, since they were remote and we rarely saw anybody when we were there. "Well, Carter was driving around up here, just exploring," he'd say. "He crossed a bridge over a river and it looked promising. So we took a canoe up there and just rowed down it. About eight miles." He was hitting his stride. "It had a good current with nice undercut banks, and it flowed into larger rivers we knew to be good. So we went back and started fishing different stretches of it. That was thirty years ago." Bass want a current that will bring food with it right in front of their protected lies, up against the bank, and even under it, where the water has eaten into the ground. This was a knowledge very few people had, and these two men cultivated it. I was lucky to know people who thought nothing of driving around for hours looking for a place to fish, and then spending a day just floating down a river to find out if it might be good enough to actually fish.

Dave had a hierarchy of fish sizes: A Good Fish was, as you would expect, good, say, sixteen inches. A *Gooood* Fish, spoken with reverence and raised eyebrows, was really good, seventeen inches or more, something to remember. A

Little Shit was a waste of everybody's time, because it was so small, the size of Dave's hand, that you could land it quickly (a large fish took time to tire out and land), and it would still have so much energy it was hard to get the popper out of its mouth. Halfway Decent was somewhere in between—say, fourteen inches—but sometimes was promoted to a Good Fish by sunset, when we were doing an inventory of the day.

We did this when we pulled out. Dave still picked the Old Town canoe up himself and hauled it onto the van, for him it was a point of pride. I had no idea how hard it was to do until I tried hoisting it on my back, and shocked at its weight, I turned too fast. The canoe turned faster. I overcompensated and staggered back and forth, fifteen-foot canoe careening over my head. I looked like a drunk giraffe. Dave had to steady me before I could rest the canoe on the van.

Fishing with somebody brings you close together because that person has a front-row seat for your failures. And those failures, if you're learning, will be frequent. As they say in baseball: The game will find you out. And no matter how well you hide, fishing knows where to find you. I made a fool of myself in front of both men countless times. Early on in my fishing with Carter, I once took my car keys out of my pocket and left them in his Ford Taurus—why would I want to carry them in the boat all day, something bad might happen? Well, the reason occurred to me when we were pulling off the river and arrived at my car, which we had left there early that morning. We were now off the river standing beside a car with no keys, the sun setting and Carter's Taurus miles upriver. Carter exhaled. This is what he got for trusting me and not using a shuttle. He went over to a man who happened to be fishing nearby and offered him $5 to drive Carter up to his car. When he returned, he said only that he would normally have yelled at the man, who had a stringer of fish he was intending to keep, illegally. That he acknowledged his proclivity to express righteous anger was refreshing.

Once that temper flared in my direction. I wasn't absolved from his ideas about the ideals of the sport. I came back from trout fishing, where it's not uncommon to strip the line in by hand (simply bringing it in with long, steady pulls instead of winding it on the reel—stripping is faster, but you lose a slight amount of control in case the fish runs). I tried to use the same approach bringing in a smallmouth bass. Carter did not approve. He erupted. "That's no way to land a fish!" It was as if John McEnroe were critiquing my backhand. Carter didn't deviate from accepted practices, I realized, and I didn't strip line in his presence again.

On balance, however, for men who took their sport seriously, both Dave and Carter were surprisingly charitable when faced with setbacks. They were taciturn among friends and perhaps their families. They might have been described as difficult men, and probably were, though they were kind to me, in their own ways, who was about the age of their grandchildren.

The first time I went out with Carter was on the lake where our families each had a cabin. The shore is lined with pines and the water is calm, deep, and very clear. He picked me up in his old Alumacraft at our wooden dock, and we slowly motored to a precise place. It was a specific time, which he chose, an hour before sunset. As the wind died down, he aligned the boat with trees on opposite shores and dropped anchor. This was not intuition and chance, this was highly calculated. He had set us up over a shelf, where the water suddenly became very deep. The bass waited for minnows to come off the edge of the shelf and then they would strike. I knew only vaguely of this invisible, underwater topography, but Carter knew it intimately. We promptly caught many. It didn't seem fair and that was Carter's intent.

It's said that 10 percent of anglers catch 90 percent of fish. This is a frightening statistic for anybody suspicious that he's not in that expert 10 percent (as with most fishing truisms, the fact that it's totally unverifiable only increases its power). Sitting there with Carter, I started to realize what it actually meant to be accomplished. Do you commit to something and do it well? Or do you do it casually and imperfectly, content not to know what you don't know? Carter didn't merely fish, he studied, experimented, refined, and nearly perfected his art. He was catching 90 percent of the fish. Did I want to catch what was left over?

The writer and fierce angler Jim Harrison said that if he was going to fish then he would only do it at a high level. I always admired this tenet even when I heard, after his death, that his angling was perhaps less technically accomplished than he let on. You can enjoy fishing at many levels, but being with Carter showed me just how high the bar was for improvement. I realized the immense amount of knowledge there was to be learned. I had impulses and vague preconceptions, it was like knowing a band's greatest hits but not their complete discography. To know a band, know their B-sides.

The angler, in Carter's view, must be learned and make informed decisions based on reason not romance. This meant years of observation on the water and reading countless books and magazines off it. He began my education by lending me *How to Fish from Top to Bottom*, Sid W. Gordon's 1955 book that Carter viewed as holy writ. He would send me articles *in the mail* to help me with my cast. Carter was deeply curious when it came to fish because he realized they would always remain elusive. It was just as impossible to have a unifying theory of music or to create a formula for making art. We could only get closer to understanding them and then try to get closer than that.

The first time I experienced something extraordinary with Carter we were on a river and I was completely unprepared. I cast to the bank as Carter had instructed. He positioned the canoe exactly as far from the bank as I could comfortably cast (I only realized the precision of this maneuver in retrospect). The popper lay by the bank and I gave it the usual little twitch. Suddenly, there was a surge of water like an anvil fell into the river. The popper was gone. I couldn't make out a fish until, miraculously, a bass jumped parallel to the water, suspended a foot clear of the surface. Its sides were dark, but its stomach was a thick strip of white. I was too stunned to speak. *What is happening?* Disoriented, I reeled in. The reel stopped. The fish had no intention of coming in. It pulled line as it tried to swim back to the bank. The tip of the rod bent and plunged with each determined run. After a few minutes, which seemed much longer, I managed to land a very good smallmouth bass, the first large one I'd ever caught. My hands shaking, I released it back into the water.

It felt like I was alone. Not just in the boat, but alone on the river, locked in a private drama. Then I remembered Carter was there. I turned to him, shocked. He had a discreet look of understanding. "Did you see that?" I managed to ask. "Yes," he laughed faintly. Of course he'd seen it. "I saw the wake." He had known the fish was coming before it had taken the popper! "Why didn't you tell me?" I was shocked he could be silent before so much excitement. "I didn't want you to overreact."

Carter had the discipline not to say anything to me, knowing it's common for anglers expecting a strike to get excited and raise the rod too soon and pull the fly right from the fish's mouth. There was also his desire, I now realize, to let me react to the situation myself and, as it happened, have a brief triumph on my own. I saw that he was happy for me and I felt I understood the nature of the game. Years later I've seen other people catch their first fish and enjoyed the sense of recognition in their eyes. So that's what this is about.

As I got to know Carter and Dave better, I could anticipate their reactions to triumphs or setbacks. A particularly well-placed cast to the bank that failed to raise a bass would have Carter exclaim, his low monotone voice slightly rising, "That cast deserved a fish!" Certain events would elicit the rare and wonderful "Sheesh!" This had multiple meanings, from aggravation to elation, depending on the behavior of the fish and the tone in which it was spoken. But mostly "sheesh" meant the surprise Carter could still feel after all these years on the water.

If we anticipated a fish along a stretch but had no action, then Dave would say, "Man, that was a good-looking bank!" For a somewhat grouchy man, Dave could be remarkably optimistic about our prospects. Also the weather. Once we were in the middle of the river in a ferocious thunderstorm and returned to the bank to wait it out. The rain had let up only slightly when Dave said, "I believe that squall has passed us by." As I noted the colloquial use of *squall*, lightning struck about fifty feet away, scaring us witless and leaving his intrepid dog Hunter quaking in the bottom of the boat.

Things go wrong when you fish, and those chances increase when you're in a boat. Often this has to do with what's known as *human error*. This is the preferred term because it doesn't name the human who made the error, especially when that human is me. Once, Dave and I were in his canoe on the last quarter mile of a long day on the water. We were around a bend from the takeout. Beyond one final rapids we would pull over and load up his van. The only thing standing in our way was a large rock. The current picked up and moved us faster, but it would be easy to avoid the rock. It would almost be harder to hit it than to miss it. I was in the bow, Dave was in the stern. Without question he was the captain, I'm not sure a fifteen-foot canoe has a captain, but Dave would be the captain of anything from a kayak to a steamer.

"Go to the left of the rock," he bellowed. This could not have been clearer and took on some urgency as the rock got nearer. Yet we rowed at cross-purposes and continued to head straight toward it. In search of clarity I shouted: "Our left or the rock's left?" The metaphysical nature of this question has remained with me over the years. If it appeared in a Basho haiku, it might be considered cryptically wise or at least a noble mistranslation.

Canoe in summer
Floats slowly down the river
Past the large rock's left

Not this time. The last thing I remember hearing, which echoed in my ears underwater as we turned over, was Dave saying emphatically, "The rock doesn't have a left!" My tendency to overanalyze simple situations was captured in this question, though I'm embarrassed to admit in private moments it still makes sense to me that a rock can have a left.

Hitting a rock with a canoe may have many reasons but one result. The canoe tipped at once, decisively, and Dave's only concern was the fate of his tackle box, which occupied a place in his spiritual landscape like the Gutenberg Bible. Thankfully, the river wasn't deep there, just a few feet. Once the tackle box was salvaged—which he always kept tightly shut in case of this exact sort of catastrophe—

Dave was in a fairly agreeable mood. He didn't care about getting wet or even mention it. He had the grin of a teenager who's just talked his way out of a speeding ticket. This was not the first canoe he'd tipped out of. He was seventy-five years old.

Much of what I learned about fishing with Dave and Carter was technical. Observing anybody who's expert at something always thrills me. Those things come with time, there's no shortcut, whether it's a sushi chef or a tailor. The brilliance hides the difficulty. I also appreciated how they shared their passion. Fishing for these men was an obsession but not mentioned in those terms. There was an alternate way of speaking, a code. Eventually I became fluent in that code.

When I first saw Dave each year, he would tell me about the trips he took to Northern Wisconsin and into Canada with his friend Louie. I never met Louie but I heard a lot about him and his great skills, with a fair amount of envy. Louie was around sixty, "a young guy," Dave said. Then Dave would ask where I'd fished since I'd seen him the previous summer. I would tell him about the Lamar River in Yellowstone National Park, about the Salmon River north of Stanley, Idaho. He would ask specific questions: what flies we used, were they all cutthroat trout, did we get out and wade. Dave had driven out to Montana every September when he was a young man and camped every night. He never saw anybody on the famous waters, he had them to himself, as he loved to point out. Those days were gone.

But he knew I was addicted and I sensed he was quietly happy about that. We shared an obsession and that meant we understood each other better. I started bonefishing in the Bahamas and he knew the lodges I went to, sometimes he even knew the guides. Now we spoke the same language. Certain phrases were mutually understood: hoppers along the bank, blue winged olives, Soda Butte Creek, Crazy Charlies, Lefty Kreh, native cutthroat. These names had meaning.

The details he wanted to know were now details I knew. When I used a light leaders and cast small flies to large trout in the spring creeks outside Livingston, Montana, he wanted to know the details. When I told him I lost a large one that broke me off he laughed. "Oh that happens," he said, like a man who knew the arc of emotions involved in love and, crucially, loss. The laugh was not at my expense. It was out of sympathy for what happens when a fish that was there is suddenly not there, as upsetting and urgent as a lightning strike. The gods have frowned upon you and it's over, the rod slack in your hand, a useless tool held by an open-mouthed man saying nothing.

In later years, Carter's health worsened and he didn't come up to the lake anymore. He lived his winter life all year round, in the South. He would write from time to time, the way my grandfather did when he was still alive, sending articles in small envelopes, with a short note, cursive handwriting from a previous era. Then those came less frequently. He didn't like hearing about fishing as much, fishing he could no longer do. When he died, his memorial service for friends from the lake was held at a bar in Bloomer, Wisconsin, the former rope-jumping capital of America, which has sadly been dislodged from that poetic distinction.

I was away and couldn't be there. I wrote something that my mom, who knew Carter most of her life, read. Carter had attended Harvard, though he never mentioned it. He was a surprising and thorough jazz enthusiast. If he was curious about something, he would study it intensely. Once I was surprised to find a William Boyd novel in his lake house and told him he was one of my favorite writers, that I was supposed to meet him in London later that year. "Well that's of interest," he said. It was one of the rare times we spoke of matters beside fishing.

As Dave got older, he would wonder if he could still make his annual trips up to Canada with Louie. These were physically demanding. "I think this past year might have been the last one," he'd say wistfully, a strong admission of vulnerability by his standards. He talked of cutting down his fishing, of trading in his beloved motorboat. This was worrying. The next summer I would call his house as soon as I arrived at our cabin, eager to fish. "May I please speak to Dave?" I asked his wife. "He's in Canada." This happened about five years in row. He couldn't give it up.

Dave's relatives would ask what we talked about while we were on the water. These were people who presumably had exhausted all other options with him at family events. "I don't know," I'd say. "Fishing. And whatever we saw." It's true, it wasn't more than that, yet it felt like more. He was an incredible naturalist who knew names of birds and trees and harvested wild rice. He knew the rhythms of seasons and where to find berries and when to pick them. We talked about those things too.

Once there's a crack in a generation it just keeps breaking. Dave died last year, at the end of a day of fishing, if you can believe it. I particularly dislike people saying the dead would want something a certain way, but Dave would have wanted it that way. In fact, he had *said* he wanted to go out fishing. Still, it was a shock.

At Dave's memorial service I finally met Louie. The trips they went on together involved camping and cooking and possessed an intensity I never quite graduated into. The service was at Dave's house on the lake; people ate venison sausage made from deer Dave had shot and drank beer from a canoe filled with ice. I was asked to tell a particular story which, to my surprise, was well known in Dave's family.

A few years earlier we were standing on his jon boat in a large river, and he caught a fish and threw the anchor overboard so we wouldn't float too far downstream while he landed it and *pass good water*. Dave would never, ever, under any circumstances, pass good water. Normally the boat would slow gently to a halt, but this time the anchor must have caught a boulder squarely because we stopped instantly. I would have fallen over the side, but I stumbled into the motor. Dave fell from the bow into the well of the boat, barely missing his dog, who moved out of the way in terror. It was thunderous. "Dave," I said. "Dave, are you all right?" He was clearly in pain and could barely speak. "My . . . my . . ." "What is it, your hip?" I asked, worried he was seriously hurt. "My rod," he gasped, "grab my rod." I took his rod, which was sliding along the edge of the boat, and landed the fish, which was still on the line. That said everything about Dave's priorities.

Louie spoke eloquently to a room full of people he barely knew. He was aware that many had been skeptical of his existence, such an invoked but un-witnessed phenomenon was he, like the mythic girlfriend from Niagara Falls. He was born in Duluth and lived in Idaho for many years, where he worked for the Department of Wildlife. He was the type of person comfortable in any outdoor situation, a kind man whose intense competence made you aware of your own inadequacies.

He was curious about me, considering that Dave and I often fished together. He said Dave had mentioned me, which was surprising somehow. It didn't seem that I would exist to Dave when we weren't on the water. Louie said, "Oh yes, he talked about you. About the trips you took." Louie paused. "He said you knew what you were doing." He smiled. Neither of us said anything more about it. We both knew what that meant coming from Dave.

MONTANA

CUTTHROAT TROUT

Assurance

I knew I had to go to Montana. It was the next step, it was that simple. Montana is the mecca of American angling and calls the faithful like the Louvre calls painters (at least painters in Henry James novels). I wanted to be around the devotees and witness their connection to the sport.

There are many ways to fish in Montana, probably

more than anyplace else. An angler can float the Beaver-head and hope to hit the Mother's Day Caddis hatch which is so thick the river looks like it's covered in late spring snow. He can nymph below the surface with tiny zebra midges in clear Armstrong Spring Creek. On cold October mornings in the Madison he can target brown trout, in their intense spawning colors, that take soft-hackle wet flies on the swing. Down a dirt road to Hebgen Lake, not far from West Yellowstone, large trout patrol the water and rise to callebaetis flies, so cast ahead of where you hear them rising. If you're lucky and intersect with the salmon fly hatch on Rock Creek on the right week in June, you'll see insects that look like prehistoric sparkplugs.

I knew none of this the first time I set out. I was possessed with the general sense that Montana was where the curious visited and the true believers lived. These people turned their lives over to the sport and then their lives became something else. They had to be near the water even if it couldn't be quantified—it had the urgency of a moral calculation. It wasn't about balance, the action justified itself. These devotees didn't come for a week, they were on the water every day and would figure out the economics later. They were flight attendants for six months so they could fish the other six. They were carpenters, ski instructors, nannies, short-order cooks, and of course they were guides. Whatever it takes to get on the water.

The water is the center of this universe and it dictates the rhythms of the day. Outfitting the drift boats, rigging up in good weather and bad, the days when the fish are everywhere and days when the fish will not turn on. Gas station coffee in the morning then bad beer that tastes perfect after landing the first trout. The weeks turn into seasons, a wider perspective and, ultimately, the long view, when it's no longer about one fish or one good day. It's the life. I didn't know the guides, the dirtbaggers, the lodge owners burning through their inheritance. I didn't know anybody. I just knew the stories. But I would meet them soon enough.

I heard stories from Dave, of course, and he was the hero of those stories. He drove out from Wisconsin each fall in the sixties to camp and fish for a month. A farmer mowed his field on a tractor, and when he came to the bank, grasshoppers jumped into the river, where large trout waited for them. Dave waited too, and he would cast hopper patterns to the bank. "Oh, that was fun," he would laugh. He told me this story every year and also reminded me that if he saw another angler on the river he would drive someplace else. It wasn't like that anymore, he cautioned me. There would be crowds.

Crowds. That ominous word. Crowds are feared at airports, St. Mark's Square, and on trout streams. The angler imagines a supposedly better, simpler past, as opposed to our far busier present. The cardinal sin is crowds. Dave made it clear that I would be sharing the water with countless others, and perhaps I shouldn't bother with Montana at all. But Montana had to be reckoned with. I wanted to witness it, to fish there and see if I felt the connection. Could I have my own stories? Could I learn what was hidden and have secrets of my own?

I decided to drive there. It was the best way, really the only way. I like driving long distances through wide open places. Driving five hours in Montana is better than five minutes in Manhattan. Just thinking about the Lincoln Tunnel makes me nervous, driving halfway across the country (if it's the Western half) is no problem.

To get to Montana from Minneapolis, where I grew up, is simple, you don't even need a map. Drive up to Fargo and turn left, then keep going straight. You can't miss it. Between Minnesota and Montana is North Dakota. You don't hear a lot about North Dakota. Maybe it's because less than a million people live there (far less) and they like to stay close to home, maybe they're self-contained by nature or their voices don't carry over the wind. But I want to put in a word for North Dakota. Don't take this the wrong way, but it's a very nice state to drive through. Highway 94 is a straight line and nothing interrupts that line. (Actually a windstorm can interrupt it. I was speeding through ND last year when out of nowhere rain arrived and then hail. I passed camper trailers that had been blown over, lifting the trucks that pulled them clear off the road.)

If you're going to have a highway going through nothing, then really commit to nothing. North Dakota goes all the way. There are few towns, no cities, no motel chains, no neon signs, no parade of billboards. Lovely wheat fields turn gold by late summer. Strings of power lines and long, lonely trains extend in the distance, like pencil marks along a ruler. Most exits promise "No Services" and are without signs of life except the occasional farmer turning slowly onto the road home.

At the western edge of the state everything falls away, the ground that was there is suddenly not there. The earth turns brown then red and the Badlands have arrived. This is where Teddy Roosevelt came after his wife and mother both died on Valentine's Day in 1884. He wanted to be alone and he knew where to go. He read, hunted, and typed letters in his tent, his boots covered in dust. Arriving as the sun sets below the canyon, there's the eerie sense of quiet that comes in vast spaces, as if a huge group of people conspired to be silent at once. I hold my breath—I don't want to make a sound.

A little farther is Montana. At first Eastern Montana is understated. This is it? There are no fishing guides handing out rods to new arrivals. It's grazing country, black Angus cows waving their tails in unison. There are no mountains and few trees. It's hot, dry, and not too green. The motel parking lots are full of workers' trucks. They arrive for seasonal jobs and drink in the saloon at night and are back in the fields early the next morning.

Poker signs glow in the windows. You can gamble anywhere in Montana: gas stations, hotel lobbies, bars, the airport. There's something intrusive coming across a person plugging coins into a slot machine, like you've found them watching pornography. Exhibitions of human frailty are better done in private.

The first big town is Miles City, more than halfway from Minneapolis to Bozeman, where I stop each time I drive out. That's maybe a dozen trips (sometimes I fly, which is too easy and never feels the same). I've stayed at the Olive Hotel every time, and every time I swear I'll never go back.

It's on Main Street and is exactly what I think I want: historic, vaguely in the Victorian style. I can imagine *Deadwood*'s infamous Al Swearengen in residence. I don't mind a hotel that has seen better days, but it's as if in 1920 the hotel said, We're the best place to stay in town, let's just relax and coast for the next century.

I've stayed in some dodgy places, which is no great claim, and some nice ones too. (Once, in Oklahoma, my motel room TV was chained to the wall, which, like many precautionary measures, was the opposite of reassuring. I got a speeding ticket leaving town the next day.) The Olive conveys the curious feeling that every room aside from yours has been condemned. There are stains in curious places—everything seems to leak. I sleep with my clothes on and go to the diner across the street, which is already full at 7 a.m., and swear I'll never return.

But waking up in Montana is a good thing. I'm happy every time that happens. The sky is big, the road is open, the world full of possibility.

I don't feel like I'm really in Montana until I see the Yellowstone, the great American river. It's wide and assured, flowing east and north with purpose. I'm embarrassed that a river flowing north seemed counterintuitive to me at first—shouldn't rivers flow down, south? That's what happens when you don't appreciate the Continental Divide.

Montana is incredibly public—you can see great distances—and yet, for me, it maintains a sense of mystery, its beauty is on full display but with something inaccessible offstage. One day I hope to inherit knowledge impossible to locate on the maps in my beloved gazetteer. I want to know places like the ones that Dave and Carter knew, with no signs and no names, places discovered and then whispered about. *Turn left at the clearing where the tree was hit by lightning. Go down to the bank and cast behind the big boulder.*

Moving west into fishing country, my pulse quickens. I pull over and look at the rivers. There are well-marked landings, with boat ramps and campgrounds, which make the basis for float trips. Each is marked with a wonderful off-white sign with pale brown lettering and a drawing of a large, leaping fish. I love these signs and their famous names: Mallard's Rest, Axtell Bridge, Grey Owl, Point of Rocks.

Farther west are mountains covered in pines, and the towns show hints of angling life. Drift boats are hitched to truck trailers or parked in front of small houses. Fly shops are down the street from other fly shops, and people walk into them still in their river clothes. Entering the stronghold, I'm instantly aware of how green I am. Guides, outfitters, and other pros make countless calculations and subtle communications. The well-worn hat from a remote Alaska lodge, the shirt from a specific company only available if you work with them—these are clues. Back then I couldn't read all of them, but I knew they were there. I knew because I had none. I was without currency.

I tried to hide behind an old hat and a beard, but I wasn't fooling anybody. There's no way to hide it. I was like a kid who had one Grateful Dead record but showed up at their show coughing through the pot smoke. The pros can tell the cork rod handle isn't stained with use, the waders are suspiciously new (Dave's were covered in duct tape, which conveyed a certain authoritative neglect). My imperfect casting felt etched across my forehead. Later, I realized you can't bluff a guide. You can pretend to know more than you do, you can make sly references and present yourself any way you want. But the guide knows, the guide always knows. It's like inhaling when a tailor measures your waist—they've got you pegged in five minutes. But that doesn't stop people from trying to hide it.

I knew roughly what to do from bass fishing in Wisconsin—same casting motion, a few of the same principles. But fishing for trout in Montana is a more delicate matter. With trout the leaders are smaller, the tippet lighter, the presentation of flies gentler. We weren't using the large poppers that could fool a bass, and in this clear water we had to abandon the heavy leaders that strong fish couldn't break. Here, the stakes were higher. A trout, especially in the current, could turn its head suddenly, and if the line was too tight there would soon be nothing but slack in the absence of that fish.

I had some vague understanding of "letting a fish run"— the fish swims away and then, at a certain point, you corral it back. I remember being equally confounded, as a child, by how, after turning the car, my dad knew how to let the steering wheel return to its correct position. Turning, I later realized, was easy, that's what power steering is for. Fly fishing has no power steering.

How did I learn this? I regret to say, suddenly and

memorably. It was my first day. I was standing with a guide below the Three Dollar Bridge, a well-known spot on the legendary Madison River. I could have floated down the river that day, but for some reason I told the guide I preferred to wade—I had an uneasy vision of myself parading down the river in a drift boat flailing a rod around, getting tangled in clear sight of everybody. This was my first mistake. If we'd floated we would have covered much more water, and it was more similar to what I did with Dave and Carter. In any case, my lack of mastery would find an audience soon enough.

So we stood there, and I have to disclose, in the interest of science, that I was not using my own rod, since I had stepped on and broken it the day before I drove out. Most embarrassing stories begin with "I never do this sort of thing . . . ," which is used precisely when you have done the thing you claim never to do. I am certainly not the type of person who would ever step on his fishing rod, except this time because I set it down on our dock for some reason, breaking the first rule: Never set a fly rod down flat on the ground—always prop it up. Which brings us to the second rule: Never prop a fly rod up near a ceiling fan. Anyway, the rod was lying down, out of sight. I took a step like any other step. I heard the faintest sound like the snapping of a toothpick in my pocket. It was barely there and yet it sounded menacing. I had stepped on the tippiest tip of the rod.

Fly rods can bend deeply and withstand an immense amount of pressure. Counterintuitively, when they are flat then they are very delicate. They don't like feet, doors, or anything that slams. Upon inspection I saw, to my horror, a slight crack. The rod-maker promised to FedEx one to the lodge in Montana where I was staying. It would arrive in two days, and be waiting for me, and that would be that. Naturally, it arrived a day after I had departed the lodge. Later in the trip I had to drive thirty minutes down the dirt road to collect it, a reminder of my ignominy.

So, as I've made clear, I was fishing by the Three Dollar Bridge with a rod that wasn't my rod. This was my first trout rod, and I had practiced extensively with it leading up to this trip. It's like cooking in a kitchen that's not your own, or wearing borrowed clothes to a party. It's essentially the same, but there's a slight lack of comfort. I'm sure Eric Clapton can play somebody else's guitar perfectly, and this is by no means a strategy of deflecting blame to the equipment and away from the user, but facts are facts.

I was fishing with a strike indicator, which is essentially a bobber. These bobbers have been re-branded with a more suitably upscale name because marketers understand that most self-satisfied fly anglers wouldn't deign to use a bobber but might use something called a strike indicator. For our purposes let's call it a bobber. The bobber, the size of a small gumball, floats in the current, letting the nymph drift in the water below it. This is a good way to catch fish since nymphs are a huge amount of what trout eat. It's not as romantic as catching a trout with a dry fly on the surface, but it's effective. If the bobber disappears in a rush, plunging down into the river, raise your rod and you have a fish. After a few hours of thrashing around that's exactly what happened. I had a trout on the line. My first Montana trout, I had arrived! I felt no fear. The fish wasn't big, on the contrary, I could barely feel it. I was in Montana connected to a fish; what could possibly go wrong?

It embarrasses me to write this because what follows is profoundly amateur, blissfully unaware. I reeled away as if the fish were on a heavy leader. This, however, was a trout on fine tackle. As the fish got nearer, I looked up and was surprised and slightly alarmed that the interloping rod was nearly bent double, further than anything I'd seen in Wisconsin. What was happening here? No small trout could bend a rod like that. This was a big fish.

In retrospect every part of this undignified story unfolded in its own way at its own pace. At the time, however, it happened at once. An experienced angler is never rushed, his actions are unhurried. Realizing that the trout was large forced my world to collapse in a second, any poise I clung to vanished downstream. I looked toward the river, and as the immense trout approached, eight feet upstream, it looked at me and I swear it made eye contact. It didn't like what it saw and it promptly broke me off. I didn't know the phrase "broke me off" at the time, which means that the fly and the fish that was on the fly were suddenly gone. The line was cleanly cut as if sliced with scissors. It was over quickly, with finality. My ears burned. What just happened?

Bob the guide, a young man with a goatee and a baseball hat, described everything he liked as "cherry," as in mint, perfect, unspeakably great. Most things that were cherry had to do with Bob and his skills and possessions. There was nothing cherry about my angling ability. "I restored a Toyota Land Cruiser," he revealed, in ecstasy. "It's so cherry, dude." After the trout and I had parted ways, I must have looked as stunned as I felt, because Bob came over and was honest enough to laugh right at me. "Dude," he said, "you should have seen your face." Well, Bob, I thought, instead of staring at my face why not give me some instruction when I clearly had no idea what I was doing? Now I had a new villain. It wasn't the rod's fault. It was Bob's fault.

One of my least favorite feelings is hearing myself say, "Why didn't anybody tell me?" This means that, whatever the situation, I've planned poorly, like being halfway through a recipe when it says, "Now set the marinade aside overnight." Oops! I meant to serve that tonight. Why didn't anybody tell me? Well actually in the recipe in fine print it does tell you right at the top. In this case the guide respected me enough not to micromanage every single thing I did when I was trying to land the fish. Why didn't he show me *less* respect?! "Don't worry, dude," Bob said. "You'll have more chances."

"It didn't feel that big," I said, when I'd gathered myself enough to analyze the disaster. "That's the current, dude. You can't always feel the fish." Since the fish was coming toward me with the current, I felt no resistance. "Well what do you do then?" I asked. "You bring it in until it decides to run. Then let it run, but keep it under control." I didn't know exactly what he meant, but I knew it was ambiguous. "And have fun with it, dude." The official fun had yet to kick in. I realize now that "have fun with it" is what guides tell beginners when the specifics seem beyond their ability.

We drove to another spot, but not before we passed the

truck of a guide that Bob knew. We pulled alongside and they discussed what was working and what wasn't. What I managed to overhear struck fear in my heart. The other guide said under his breath that there were "some limitations" and nodded toward the group of unknowing anglers, out of earshot, in a state of oblivion in the backseat while their skills were slandered up front.

Limitations. This concerned me. I thought guides weren't supposed to discuss their "sports," in the traditional parlance. There was a code, a doctor/patient privilege that guides followed. Would Bob be telling his fellow guides at the bar tonight about my shortcomings? "You should have seen his face, dude, he just reeled right in and it broke him off. What do you expect? He lives in New York." It was true humiliation, like people watching a video of you dancing.

Here's how my day ended with Bob. I took the proverbial last cast. Now, with a guide this is different than when you're on your own or with a friend. The day usually ends at 5 p.m. or some given time—you're on the clock. There's not a lot of wiggle room. Men on their own, and it is usually men who are so irrational and stubborn, often keep fishing past the hour they said they would and arriving cold and wet and in the dark well into the dinner hour.

Actually, I had taken a few last casts and took one more. Please don't think this happens or you'll be making far too many last casts (but we all make too many last casts). A last cast is being down three runs in the bottom of the ninth against a good closer. I'm sure the analytics crowd has come up with a percentage for how often the home team wins. But you're not catching a fish on your last cast often. In this case, however, the bobber plunged, a fish was on. Another big trout. *I'm redeemed,* I thought. *The fishing gods love me and recognize my worth. Nothing can stop me, not Bob, not this rod. I'm the chosen one!*

Now the story would have its happy ending. I learned my lesson from the morning and I wouldn't reel in too quickly. This trout wanted to run and I would let it. It wanted to swim upstream and that was all right. I could feel its weight. I was *having fun with it.* Well I wasn't exactly having fun, I was just trying to avert disaster. I wouldn't reel it in aggressively like the novice of this morning. I scoffed at that version of myself. I understood the stakes and for a minute it was fine. The problem was that I was having too much fun with it. A lot of line was out, I had let it run too far and lost control. *Why didn't anybody tell me?* If a trout goes too far out, you have to turn it back, but when it's big that's hard to do. Well, a more experienced angler could do it, but not me. The fish was gone. This time the fish broke off not from me being aggressive but from me being passive. The fun was over, like a high school party broken up by the cops.

The sound of me swearing echoed along the banks of the Madison, and other anglers who dotted the far side of the river looked up. "Sorry," I said under my breath, but only Bob could hear. "Don't worry about them, dude. They're assholes anyway."

Important things are learned through failure, or at least through experience. If they didn't have to be learned, they wouldn't be worth knowing. Fighting a fish is one of those things. It wasn't Bob's fault, and in a weird way it wasn't mine. It was part of my education. Looking back on it is like reading a high school essay. Or worse, a junior high school essay. You know what the young version of you is trying to say, but you just didn't have the right language. Trying to land a big trout doesn't make sense until you go through it a number of times. When you learn one lesson, then you realize there's something else to learn, which is usually learned in the tragic aftermath of a lost fish.

A trout wants to do things, and you can allow it to do some of those things and not others. I suspect this is how it feels to be the parent of a teenager (I have the deep knowledge of somebody with no children). You allow the fish to seem in control without it really being in control. Your authority is hidden, but in fact you're guiding it. When I fight a fish now, I know what it is trying to do and I know what I'm trying to do. That doesn't mean I don't lose fish, but it does mean I usually lose them on my own terms.

Here are some general rules (yes there are exceptions!) that help land fish.

- *Apply pressure.* Keep the line tight. Slack line makes it far easier for a trout (or any fish for that matter) to shake the hook loose.
- *Keep the fish upstream.* Fish swimming against the current will tire far more quickly. If it gets downstream and swims with the current, it can be hard to turn it back toward you.
- *Don't let it run and run.* "Having fun" aside, I like to

land fish quickly. The longer a fish is running, the
more things that can go wrong.
- *Be prepared for runs.* Especially when a fish sees a
person, a boat, or a net, it will make a last dash. If
it tries to swim away from you, point your rod at it
and be prepared to let some line out.
- *Land the fish out of the current.* It's much easier
to manage a fish in slower water, especially when
you're trying to land it. You might have to wade
back toward the shore.

My Montana education began with losing fish on the banks
of the Madison—though I've refined it by losing them on
other storied rivers and streams as well. I learned things I
never thought to ask: That it's impossible to find a hotel
room a hundred miles in any direction when Evel Knievel's
son's car show is on. His name is Robbie, but most people
call him Evel Knievel's son. Or that Montana diners bless-
edly serve hash browns, which are delightful, as opposed
to the dreaded, soggy home fries back on the East Coast.
These same diners also serve cream with coffee when you
ask for milk. Even when they say it's milk, it's still cream.

I always start my trip by buying a license (which still
lists my weight from when I bought it, twenty years ago,
which is a bit of an eye opener). It's possible to do this
online now, but I like to go into the old Dan Bailey store, in
Livingston, with its illustrated tracings of large trout covering the walls.

When was the last time you bought a jazz compact disc?

Try it, it's fun. Go to Vargo's Jazz City & Books on Main Street in Bozeman. I usually buy one because I like the handwritten description by the owner. If I'm in the area, I try to head to the Missoula green market on Saturday mornings. In early June one year I bought morels at a good price from a man with a long, gray beard. He had two tables covered with nothing but morels. I asked where he got them. He squinted and looked at me and, as vague as any angler about his secret fishing spot, said simply, "On the border with Idaho," an area more than three hundred miles long.

Education can be ennobling and it can be defeating. You only have to learn certain things once. Don't be foolish and walk in your waders up to Slough Creek. I headed up the steep hill in Yellowstone around 11 a.m., and it's quite a climb, and I timed it perfectly wrong and arrived on the water fully perspired right at noon when the sun was bright (which the fish don't like) and the water was warm (again: unpopular with trout). I passed more expert anglers who were already on their way down the hill (they'd arrived early in the morning when the fishing was good). They also *packed* their waders, like any sane person. Another moment which will live in infamy.

To me, being in Montana means driving long distances, and I love being on the road there. I drive too far to go fishing and then too far to look for lodging. At this point I've developed a mental map with places to stay. That map includes the Lewis & Clark Motel in Bozeman, with a large neon sign of the explorers out front and banana bread in the lobby every morning.

There's Chico Hot Springs. An institution off Highway 89 near Pray (what a name for a town) on the way to Yellowstone. It's got some fancy suites, but I've stayed in singles in the main lodge, old rooms that don't have bathrooms, when the trips were long and funds were low. I prefer the rustic cabins, which feel like they haven't changed since the 1950s and probably haven't.

Everybody should visit the Sportsman Motel in Melrose, which is legendary as far as I'm concerned. A one-story strip motel, the classic setup, very clean and well run. They advertise that they have free ice, and leave a handwritten note on the office door around 5 p.m. saying that the owners can be found in a bar down the street.

There are remote places where you don't want to arrive at night. Like the very small cabin behind a Mexican restaurant that was the only room I could find after some terrible planning on Labor Day. There are also cabins, in a dive motel in Lincoln, with curious, almost psychedelically patterned décor. I learned later it was the town where the Unabomber was apprehended. At the other end of the spectrum, which is really like the other end of the universe, is the Ranch at Rock Creek, one of the most elegant hotels in America, whose chef is an amazing, accomplished man named Josh. I'm not sure any of the other hotels has a chef.

Drive south along Highway 89 through Paradise Valley, through Jim Bridger Canyon, and you'll get to Gardiner, the last town before the north entrance to Yellowstone National Park. Stop by Parks' Fly Shop, which has been there since the 1950s, where Dave used to buy flies. There's a serviceable saloon—as at many places, the food is good for breakfast and gets progressively worse over the course of the day. There's a self-service laundromat and shops that sell candy to tourists bribing their children with sugar.

Yellowstone is one of America's great settings, and it took a fight when it was founded in 1872 to set the land aside and protect it for the public. Timber interests and developers wanted to keep it private. Imagine that. It's one of the true legacies in our country and a special place to be. I love the smart ranger uniforms and the rows of wood houses where they stay, the carved signs with wonderful fonts and the civilized post office. But the real thing is the landscape and the animals who live there.

There are bison, of course. At first they're far away, dotting the fields, grazing in herds. Then they get closer, possibly too close. A large one decides to enter the road and walk right down it, and suddenly he's leading a slow parade of cars. Last year a bison walked toward my car, and traffic parted to let it through. There's no shoulder on the road, so I couldn't clear out of the way. It was right next to me—if it had swung its mighty head around it would have knocked off my rearview mirror and worse. This was a new car, by the way, and I was actively hoping not to have that happen. I had, in fact, just traded my old car, a beloved Saab, for a fishing rod, which is a different story altogether.

The only reason I have a car is so I can drive places to fish. Alas, Saab is no longer, but I remain partial to Swedish cars. So I tracked down a Volvo wagon with the intention of converting it into a mobile storage unit devoted to angling. The way back is divided with the precision of a bento box. Over the years it's been refined with a mix of the personal and scientific, according to the needs of this traveling angler—bags are stacked and packed so precisely that I hesitate to let anybody else have access to *The Storage System.* I may not be able to find last year's tax returns in my apartment, but I can find an ancient map of Silver Creek in my car in no time.

Starting in the trunk is a back row, divided into three parts.

- *Rear (Left):* A YETI cooler I received as a gift from a friend who works there, who has one of the world's better jobs. As far as I can tell he goes on photo shoots with the serious anglers and chefs the company partners with (he fishes and eats *very* well). It's possible he feels guilty about his good luck and gave me this cooler out of pity, which is fine with me. It's filled with enough ice for two days and enough beer for a week. Possibly lunch.
- *Rear (Middle):* Next to the cooler is a cardboard box. I have a propensity for Leinenkugel's, the terrifically mediocre beer I grew up on in summers in Wisconsin. Well, old cardboard Leinenkugel's cases are the perfect size for good storage. The cases had to be sturdy enough because you filled them with empty bottles that you returned when you bought your next case, so you didn't have to pay the deposit again. This box carries hats—baseball hats, hats with brims, good luck hats, hats for when I'm desperate. At least four. There are also a few things that come

in handy—a small towel, a couple of extra water bottles, an empty cigar box, a laundry bag.

- *Rear (Right):* Another Leinenkugel's case carries old Simms wading boots, and other shoes I might need—canvas slip-ons, a pair of L.L. Bean boots, and some neoprene wading socks, in case I'm not wearing waders.
- *Front (Left):* One of those wonderful old, boxy Air Force kit bags, faded green canvas. I buy them when I find them cheap. I got this one from a roadside military surplus expo (if that's the word) in the Utah desert where most of my fellow shoppers had spent more time with heavy firearms than I had. This one is full of cold weather clothes—a heavy cardigan, a wool overshirt, a lined khaki shirt that's easy to fish in. Some plaid shirts, a Patagonia parka.
- *Front (Middle):* A duffel, this one is a particular tan canvas model made in St. Paul, Minnesota, in the 1980s by a company that's underpriced on eBay. In it are fishing shirts—tan button-ups, a white, a green, maybe an odd muted yellow chamois. A few pairs of chinos.
- *Front (Right):* A ventilated Orvis bag for waders and rain jackets. I have two of each, for some reason. I'm sure the reason is good.

Tucked on the side are rod tubes and a net. Set on top of all of this is a bag that contains all the fly boxes, reels, and what I wear when I wade. There's a Filson jacket. There's a brown tweed herringbone sport coat, in case the lodge I'm staying at is nice.

- *In the Car:* Bottle opener, lighter, corkscrew, wooden fork. Tom Petty *Greatest Hits* CD. Business cards of my favorite fly shops. An extra pair of sunglasses. A small, very durable glass that's the rare size and shape that makes it acceptable for both whiskey and wine. I am very particular about this glass.
- *Behind the Driver's Seat:* A box of Snyder's of Hanover classic sourdough pretzels. The big pretzels. The brown box. Not easy to find. I buy at least two boxes whenever I come across them, which is occasionally at Albertsons in Livingston. The perfect food when you're without food.
- *Behind the Passenger Seat:* The empty cardboard box a Miller Lite twelve-pack comes in (the beer's in the cooler). I drink bottles of Leinenkugel's for nostalgic reasons at our cabin, I drink cans of Miller Lite when fishing. Don't think of it as bad beer, think of it as good water. This box is for trash and recycling. I like the car to be clean. It imparts order and clarity of mind, not unlike a well-organized fly box. (I spend far too long organizing my fly boxes into morale-building straight and logical rows. I do that with my bookshelves too. This might be a condition of some kind.)

The idea is that I will always be ready for a . . . *fishing emergency*. If I get the call, like some angling superhero or a fishing fireman, I'm ready to be on the water right away.

Does this happen often? It does not. Do I fantasize about it happening? Constantly. But a well-ordered car makes it easy to find what I need if I'm parked by the river. I thought I was slightly obsessive about this, but then I visited Taite, a friend who guides in Idaho. He packed his perfectly maintained 1980s Land Cruiser in the most precise way possible. Taite, I noted with some interest, is an adherent of the *Bin System*. I respect his dedication and rigor and felt slightly vindicated, or at least that I had a fellow traveler.

There are so many beautiful settings within the park that it's absurd to have a favorite, but my favorite is the Lamar Valley. In the base of the valley is Soda Butte Creek, which, since it's easy to wade and is near the road, is a popular place to fish. I usually park there and walk across the valley, over a hill, and down to the Lamar River.

I don't know if analyzing why we respond to a natural setting diminishes its mystique. It's like trying to figure out why a joke is funny—better to laugh at Jacques Tati and just enjoy it. But I have a weakness for large, wide open spaces with bluffs in the distance. There's room to move, while the hills provide perspective. I like feeling small, even insignificant, in a beautiful place. It's humbling and somehow correct. That's the case in the Lamar Valley. The fishing is almost secondary. But it's never secondary because I want to catch a trout in this special place. I'm always excited to fish the Lamar. I remember exactly where I once caught a large cutthroat one warm day, and it felt like a good omen to return to the same place.

THE OPTIMIST

As Americans the cutthroat trout is our native fish. It's at home in the clean cold waters of the Mountain West. It derives its name from the slash of vivid orange (not quite red to my eye) along its jaw. I think of it as a gold and dusty pink fish. More stunning and regal than the rainbow trout and not quite as mercurial as the elusive brown trout.

The cutthroat trout is the state fish of Idaho, of Wyoming, and of Montana. Which gives a sense of where these fish are found and also a reminder that it's nice for states to have a state fish. I love the black spots on the sides of cutthroat trout. Their spacing is quite varied and random. Sometimes there are a lot, but often there aren't too many, as if the fish got tired and didn't get dressed up all the way. Muted gold often dominates the background, like a rich streak of lacquer, something precious and rare.

On my way to try to catch a cutthroat I come to a sign on the dirt path that says the entire area is closed because a grizzly bear has been reported in the area. I don't like the sound of a bear, but I really don't like the sound of not fishing. Clouds arrive and with them rain. I turn to an accepted path that leads upstream away from my usual spot. Walking in waders and rain gear is not fun. Rain makes the proceedings even less fun, a humid situation inside and out. After a slog, I arrive at the river, in a place where the bank is deep and difficult to wade. There are trees and brush and it's a pain in the ass. To make matters worse, after all that, there's the bear I dutifully tried to avoid, bent over on the other side of the river. I'm trying to decide how scared I should be and if bears can swim across rivers, when it turns around and reveals itself to be a bison. I should have been better able to determine one hairy brown backside from another. Good grief.

Sometimes it's just not happening and you have to admit you're licked. The water is off-color and too high, the conditions aren't right. The fact that I hiked a long way entitles me to nothing. I have to accept that there's no way to catch a good fish here. I'm out. I head back to the car. I trekked (well it was a hike, but let's call it a trek) to a place where I couldn't catch a fish, and now I have to trek back in the rain. Things can't get worse. But I spoke too soon. An angler should know that there's always the threat of deeper embarrassment to come. Things can always get worse.

Standing in my way is a hill of mud, maybe twenty feet tall. I can't make it up the hill, even though I'm wearing studded boots, which should help. But the greatest physics experts in Greece (or wherever they invented gravity) couldn't have devised a less agreeable angle of mud for me to climb. As reality sets in, I'm even madder at my inability to scale this small hill, especially after going trout-less on the Lamar. In the name of anglers everywhere I will climb this mud hill. It's a point of principle. I try to sidle up it, as if not looking at it directly will give me the advantage of stealth. I slide back down. I give myself space and get a running start. Nada. It's too stupid, but it's even more stupid to fail. I'll have to retrace my steps ten, fifteen minutes at the most, which is not too bad, a half hour total. Like an absolute child, I'm stuck in a battle of wills with Mud Mountain.

By the time I retreat, I've given serious consideration to snapping my rod in half. The fly rod's incredible fragility makes it a constant temptation to the angler's temper. It's always at hand, and I've nearly broken one over my knee on countless shameful occasions, but have always held out. There's a strange moment when things go so wrong and you finally give yourself the liberty to laugh at them. If the day's going south, then by all means go all the way south, bomb out, live to tell the tale, then tell it.

So I have to walk an extra thirty minutes. As I like to say after an appalling day fishing, *at least we weren't hit by lightning*. Because that really is the worst thing that can happen—and that's a story people *will* listen to. My mind is clouded as the rain lets up and I finally approach Soda Butte Creek. I'm soaking. I should go back to the car, which is close by, and change into something dry. But the weather has cleared the park, and I have the famous water to myself. Why not wet the line? Things can only get better—actually that's not true. They could maintain this unrivaled level of worseness.

But my luck feels like it has turned along with the weather. The sun comes out and little mayflies hatch along the stream. I stand on a bank where the water snakes into a bend and fish are waiting to eat. I can see their noses barely poking up to take small flies. It's always amazing when a stream comes alive as if there's a charge in it. The fish begin feeding at once. It's also a reminder of just how many fish there are, which is either reassuring to know they're there or infuriating to know how hard it is to catch them.

After all the absurdities of the day I try to stay calm and take my time tying on a small gray Adams fly, the size of a sunflower seed, which imitates the hatch. I wandered for hours and saw no good fish, and now there are many of them minutes from where I parked. Go figure. The current brings the fly right into the bank, where a trout comes to meet it. I have a strong, lovely cutthroat trout on the line. The water is narrow, and I can keep it under control. I'm ready when the fish tries to make its run, and I let it go, but not too far. I sense when the trout tires and start to strip line in. I bring it in close and carefully net it. A gold head gives way to a side striped with deep pink. A perfect fish. I let it go and look around. It's still daylight. Fish are rising. I laugh out loud. Nobody's there to hear me.

BAHAMAS

BONEFISH

Vision

Airports in the Bahamas are too big or too small. They can be oversize and half-empty like shopping malls about to go bankrupt. Sun-stained travelers parade slowly past stands selling rum cake. It's not unknown for people to miss connecting flights as they tuck into another daiquiri, trusting they'll hear an announcement that doesn't penetrate the bar's interior.

Then there are airports that aren't really airports at all, just small buildings with a desk and some plastic chairs next to a runway that you didn't even realize was a runway until a small pastel-colored plane landed on it. A woman sells coffee from behind a small counter, and her friends stop by to gossip. There's a vending machine with obscure junk food nobody's seen since the eighties, if ever.

In Nassau it goes from very large to very small, and in between is a touch of the surreal. Arriving at the international airport, you're greeted by a pirate. He stands, in costume, mustached, eye-patched, talking to a security guard until he sees passengers coming around the corner and gets into character. This is not method acting. "Welcome to Nassau! Have a good time now!" Then he makes a guttural growl that sounds like a lion swallowing a beer bottle. You wait to get your passport stamped in a room with a steel-drum band performing at half speed. My belief is that if there's entertainment anywhere you're in line, then that line will not move fast. In Nassau, my belief isn't tested.

The small airport for charter flights to outer islands is a few minutes away. It's a lounge with outdated black leather furniture (though all black leather furniture is outdated) and a surprising number of magazines about private air travel, a category, in my naïveté, I hadn't realized existed. It's mostly listings of used planes for sale, and it's interesting to examine different eras and their prevailing styles of bad taste. Some planes look slightly official as if they belonged to fleeing dictators, others more ostentatious, for ferrying moguls to weekend homes and private islands. All possess the air of a once-promising investment gone wrong.

The prevailing mood in this lounge depends on the weather. Flights have to leave by mid-afternoon because outer island airports have no towers or runway lights, the planes have no instruments. Without getting too technical, the runway is a strip of pavement surrounded by dying grass and a chain-link fence any ten-year-old could climb over, though there's no reason to. You have to land well before dark sets, so the plane can take off again, and that's that. You can't negotiate with the sunset.

Our group, just arrived from New York, surveyed the weather. It didn't look good. Somebody heard something from another group who had their own source of intelligence, and one thing was clear: If we didn't take off soon, we'd lose our window to leave and spend the night in Nassau. In short, we'd lose our first day of fishing in Andros. To be so close to the action and then have to retreat to some resort, presumably with its own pirate to greet us, was a tough situation. Those that had travel insurance kept asking the rest of us if we had it, which didn't endear them to us. When you're asked if you have travel insurance, it's always too late.

After huddling with the man who seemed to be in charge, we discovered the charter airline was contacting another pilot—it was unclear what had happened to pilot number one. It was a weekend afternoon, our new man was at a nearby picnic, they called his cell phone, and a price was agreed upon. We were in no position to be demanding, and he agreed to come right over and fly us the thirty minutes to Andros.

I never realized how much authority a uniform confers until we got into a plane with a pilot whose knees were visible—he wore shorts and a striped polo shirt. All of this unfolded against the backdrop of my healthy suspicion of small planes. The more remote the destination, the less my sense of faith. The plane we boarded wasn't featured in the private airline magazine. If it belonged to a dictator, that dictator was deposed decades ago. The interior featured an unsettling amount of duct tape. I'm not sure if it's worse that the plane—which had a brown-and-green color scheme dating from the 1970s—needed duct tape or that what they'd decided was wrong with it could be fixed with duct tape.

Duct tape is a universal solution, both authoritative and innocent. That problem is taken care of, it announces, with the satisfaction that comes with simple solutions. But how long the duct tape solved the plane's problem was not something I wanted to find out at altitude. It reminded me of the unnerving feeling once on a much larger plane when the pilot came over the speaker to inform us that there was something wrong with the plane's electrical system so he was turning the power off and then back on again. I didn't like the sound of that, since it was exactly how I try to fix anything with an on/off switch. Turning something off and on is the electronic version of applying duct tape. When it comes to planes, I prefer solutions I wouldn't have thought of myself.

But here we were, in a taped-up plane, with a pilot who looked like a college student, racing the clock to take off. The cabin was the size of a station wagon, and duffel bags covered every inch of interior space. Somebody's ancient canvas rod case, nearly five feet long, was lodged into my lap so I couldn't move one way or the other. A light on the plane's dash flashed an insistent red. Since nobody mentioned it (one member of our group was himself a pilot), I didn't want to ask if this alarmed anybody else. We pulled onto the runway.

As we gained speed, the pilot turned around and asked in a remarkably casual tone, "You guys are going to Andros, right?"

If you've been to Andros, you probably were there to fish. You might remember that one side of the island is trees and vegetation, while the other is a beach and small houses, and they're divided by a road. It's very straightforward. From the air, the water is translucent near the island, pale blue like a sapphire. It doesn't get darker until much farther out. These light, shallow expanses are the flats. Bonefish feed on the flats, and we're here to catch bonefish.

I'm here by accident. My friend Markley arranged the trip, and one of his friends dropped out, so I replaced him at the last minute. "I don't want to pressure you," Markley said like a character in a Whit Stillman film. "But you should really come." Before I responded, he added, "In fact, it would be crazy if you didn't." That felt like pressure. This was a trip with serious anglers who knew the terrain and one another. I had met none of them except Markley.

Like Dave, Markley grew up fishing with his father and grandfather. And, like Dave, he has the easy sense of expertise that comes with doing something one's whole life, like those infuriating people who learned perfect French as a child. But where Dave was overt and declarative, Markley is a reluctant angling philosopher. He's skeptical of the poetic elements of the sport and would not, for example, read a book on fly fishing. "I don't like them," he says, shortly. "Unless they're instructive," he clarifies. His interests are technical and scientific—he's more likely to study a magazine devoted to carp fishing in England than an ode to the sport.

Markley and I love old fishing clothes—the canvas and waxed cotton that his grandfather wore—and I send him eBay listings when I find old boots and Barbour wading jackets. But Markley will hike two hours uphill to catch small, native fish. This is where we part company—if I'm spending hours getting somewhere, I want the possibility of catching something memorable. That's because I haven't gravitated to the next level of enlightenment, Markley implies. "You wouldn't like it," he tells me, about a remote stream. "There's nothing big enough for you." The level of disdain is noticeable. "I don't need to catch large fish," I insist. "I just don't want to catch eight-inch fish." "But small fish on a mountain stream are the best!" he insists. It's good to have a friend like Markley; you can discuss these vital matters and refine your attitudes over time.

My misgivings about this trip have to do with the fishing. This wasn't a road trip to Montana pursuing my beloved trout. This was flying to the Bahamas for a fish I'd never seen before. This meant new rods, new reels, new flies, new strategies, and, crucially, new ways to embarrass myself. I had visions of catching nothing, of returning home in shame. You went to Bahamas to go fishing? I imagined friends asking, assuming that if I went all that way it must have been great, amazing, downright historic. What if I was sunburned but shut out? What if I caught nada, bubkes, the big zip?

I remember Dave telling me about a fishing trip when not only did they not catch fish, they barely even *went* fishing. "The goddamn wind blew us out!" he howled. "It just blew us out." He was still mad about it. In retaliation, he returned a month later. It was a short flight and he lived in Florida in the winter. Anglers like to exact revenge, every unraveled trip bitterly remembered in great detail. I'd have no recourse. I had one chance, this was it. And not to put too fine a point on it, but there's nothing else to do on this part of Andros—you can't swim (the flats are too shallow and too long). You're there for the fish and the fish alone.

But saltwater fishing was another step in my angling education. Following the fishing calendar, I began to realize, means heading south when the snow arrives, like geese or retirees. Fly fishing in the winter steers the opportunist to the Bahamas for bonefish. We weren't in Montana anymore. No waders, no drift boats, no trees. Skiffs and sight fishing in flats looking for big, strong fish. Visions of heat, salt, and blue water swirled in my mind as I booked a ticket to Andros.

I'd heard about bonefishing, whispers here and there. I knew it depended on the wind and the sun. The angler needs the sun to see the fish, but not too much wind to make casting impossible. Clouds turn the water opaque, and then you can't see the fish or the shadows of the fish. Seeing bonefish is everything, since you only cast to a fish you see—there's no speculation. You can go an hour without casting, which doesn't make for a good advertisement for bonefish. But what you do hear is that when a bonefish takes the fly it goes on a screaming run, swimming away at high speed, pulling out line. It's a mighty fish for its size. People who bonefish become obsessed with it.

But could I handle another obsession? Did my heart have room for the bonefish? On a logistical level, could I even fit more rods, reels, and boots in my apartment? Wasn't my head too addled to strategize about a new fish that lived far away from New York? Could I learn the famous saltwater fly patterns like Crazy Charlie, the Gotcha, and all the other crabs and shrimp?

To make matters more complicated, the bonefish is not classically attractive. There are not poems penned on the bonefish. Taxidermists are not backed up with bonefish waiting to be mounted for studies and bars. The bonefish lacks the nobility of the trout or the majesty of the salmon, which may be why you haven't heard of it. But if you have, then you're aware of its intense appeal, which has to be experienced firsthand, like the rodeo or experimental theater.

Known as the silver phantom, in the water the bonefish is nearly translucent and hard to see. Its large eyes give it, to my mind, a sweetly innocent look, as if it's constantly startled. And bonefish is indeed easily spooked—it doesn't enjoy surprises, like shadows, sound, or sharks. Its mouth is on the bottom of its head, like a carp's. It is not technically beautiful, you won't fall in love when you see its photo. But I didn't know the bonefish yet. And bonefish, I learned, grow on you.

What I also learned, and have learned subsequently, is

that there's always room in the angler's life for a new obsession. We may try to protect ourselves from another passion, and then a trusted friend says, *Yes, it's worth a decade
of insane devotion*—which is exactly what we wanted to
hear in the first place. The next thing you know you're in
the Bahamas with Markley.

Andros means *male* in Greek, which is fitting since the lodge
guests are, indeed, mostly men. To underline the situation,
the lodge website specifies that there are *"no* non-angling
activities." This means that you're not to bring friends or
family, who understandably would expect to relax by a pool
or beach while you're out struggling to see a bonefish. No,
this will not be a vacation that satisfies both halves of a couple
unless both halves fish. It is for anglers and anglers only.

In Andros, the morning light is even and gray. The air
has that gentle weight, which always surprises me in the
Caribbean. It's mild and welcomes you outside. The first
question is about the wind: Is it going to pick up or lie
down? Nobody really knows. It's just men guessing while
trying to sound authoritative, which is a lot of fishing. It
makes fleeting experts of us all.

"If it stays like this, we should be fine," someone says.
"Coming from the north," another observes. "That could
mean a front." My experience with fronts, particularly cold
fronts, is that they're never good—which I realize is my way
of trying to sound authoritative. What we want in the flats
is a light breeze at most—and we want sun. But it all feels
unknown to me. Despite the out-of-print books I've tracked

down and read, I still can't imagine what to expect. We're assigned our guide for the day. Markley and I will be with Pap, who, the lodge owner tells us, is a man of few words. As men of many words this causes us great intrigue. Markley and I speculate about whether Pap, in his silence, will be philosophical, distant, or judgmental. Perhaps all three.

Our group climbs onto the back of a truck which is fighting a losing battle against rust. We ride a short five minutes to the dock and get out to see four flats boats rolling gently in the water. The guides stand easily in the back. It's the first morning in a new place and a new type of fishing, and I feel anxious like it's the first day of school. The guides are the teachers who've seen anglers come before us and will see them after we've gone. They are the true experts who know about the sun and wind and tides. They chatter among themselves in an impenetrable dialect, finalizing their strategies for the day.

The boats have just been cleaned, the tanks filled with gas, the coolers packed with ice. The sun, barely visible over a few reluctant palms, reflects off the white hulls. Pap has a sweet bearing, a gentleness like a Buddha and something that we rarely recognize—he's shy. We hand our rods over to him, and he carefully stows them in recessed holders under the gunwales. Markley and I get on board and sit on a narrow, white leatherette bench. Pap stands behind us, steering from the console. We slowly back up and pull away from the dock.

There are many things I love about the morning before fishing begins. The day is still perfect, faultless, like a relationship before the first fight. This is all magnified on the

Bahamas flats, where the air and light are so lovely. We move alone on the water, speeding south. All the thinking and the overthinking vanishes. The neuroses and worrying burn away. This is not theoretical, it's pure motion and joyous.

The boat feels like it's floating above the water. A flats skiff is a white slab, a Kevlar hull covered in resin, brilliantly designed to go at high speed in shallow water. And by shallow I mean shallow. Twenty inches, less. Speeding in a few feet of water, however, can be unnerving when a hidden bank of coral presents itself suddenly. But we have faith in Pap, the man of few words. In fact, we are in his hands in many ways. He's our transport, but just as crucially, he's our eyes.

We head toward the southern edge of the island. The shore is mangroves and coral. The highest point is a stunted six-foot palm tree where an opportunistic osprey has built its nest, like an immense crown of thorns. We speed over shadows that reveal themselves as sea turtles and rays swimming languidly beneath us. Nothing is in a rush except us. The motor is loud and tears stream from my eyes in the wind. After twenty minutes we come around the narrow tip of the island. Pap cuts the engine. Silence descends as the boat glides to a stop. We are on our first flat. The sun is up.

What I saw from the shore of the camp hasn't prepared me for this. As far as you can see, farther than you can imagine, the flats are wide open, endless. It feels like we're the only people on earth. I've never felt as wonderfully isolated and remote. Sand and water, the palest blue and brown, meet in endless silver slivers. The horizon extends in every direction interrupted by lines of mangroves. This is a wild place, like the desert. But the desert is unforgiving and the flats feel reassuring. There are more elements, more possibility.

Pap climbs on the poling platform in the back of the boat. It's three or four feet higher. He pushes us in silence with an eighteen-foot pole. Enough speculating and admiring. It's time for action. Let's fish. Poetry has to be intruded upon with a moment of angling inspiration and possibly embarrassment. Markley suggests I go first, and to get over my nervousness I agree. Might as well get down to it. I climb up onto the bow, it feels like a stage and time for the soliloquy I haven't memorized. With two anglers, one stays down in the well to watch, offer moral support, or pretend he didn't see the other do something foolish. He does this with a combination of professional interest, schadenfreude, and, if the fishing is good, mild jealousy.

So here I am, fishing before Pap, Markley, and the angling gods for a fish I can't see. It's nothing like trout or bass fishing, where you cast again and again, which helps you get a rhythm. When you finally see a bonefish, then, and only then, will you make a cast, so it better be good, or all that waiting was for nothing. When you've never seen a bonefish before, they're even more difficult to see. I knew this ahead of the trip and read books and watched videos in preparation for this moment. I stared at photographs with the intensity of a conspiracy theorist watching the Zapruder film. It's not enough.

And, like a schoolboy wearing his new clothes on the first day, I am outfitted with a new reel. Normally, I frown upon anything too gleaming, especially when it comes to clothes, but also rods, reels, and tackle. You want your waders to be scarred from use, not fresh and unworn. Fred Astaire had his valet (his *valet*!) throw his suits against the wall to take the newness out of them. This isn't the same thing exactly, but gleaming, unused equipment on the flats just reinforces my lack of experience.

But this is my saltwater debut, and I made some late-night online investments in a reel. And, naturally, a backup reel, because who knows what might happen and also I'm insane. The saltwater reel is an object of fascination, and it takes on an outsized importance on the flats. A trout reel is small and, though coveted, does not need to be any different than your grandfather's reel. In fact it might be your grandfather's reel. Owners of reels, especially those that are inherited, often find them hard to let go of. The objects come to represent the passions of the original owner, and that is worthy of reverence, even if that reverence stays in the back of a desk drawer.

In the salt, the reel is larger and so is its significance. When a bonefish is on the line, he tears, and I mean tears, 150 yards into the distance at 20 mph, about the speed of a cheetah. You're going to get to know your reel very well at that point. It makes a loud metallic whirl that can't be imitated or reproduced. Only a fish on the line can make it, so you'll come to love that sound. If you try to stop the bonefish from running, then the fly will break off instantly. To put this in perspective, the speed that a bonefish takes off can cause the reel (spinning in reverse) to break a thumb that gets in the handle's way. This is light tackle fishing after all. Nobody said it was easy, nobody even said it was logical. But many beautiful things place principles over logic.

Reeling in is easy. Releasing line as if it's attached to a speeding motorbike is another matter. Reel companies are proud of their drag, a system that controls the tension at which the line can be released. The drag has to be set correctly, which happens by turning a knob on the reel, forward or backward, to tighten or loosen it. If the drag is too loose, the line comes out too quickly and the speeding bonefish will twist the line into an infernal tangle. Too tight, and the pressure from the fish will break the fly off. A nice, steady, slow pull should work. Adjusting this while gazing meaningfully into the distance is another chance for the angler to make himself feel like an expert. The reel may be designed to handle the stress of the moment the bonefish runs, but the question is whether the angler can handle the stress of that moment.

Part of the art of casting is getting close enough that the bonefish sees the fly but not so close that when the fly lands the splash spooks it. Bonefish are eager to eat but quick to flee. In theory you cast near the fish and then pull in line in short strips to imitate a darting shrimp. If the fly doesn't move, it looks unnatural and the bonefish loses interest. Beginners like myself take more instruction from the guide, who stands on the poling platform, where he pushes the boat silently and has the best vantage point. He's been looking for bonefish for decades. Pap, an Andros native, focuses his silence on the horizon and scans for signs of life.

We're fishing a Gotcha, a well-known fly that looks like a shrimp. It's a few shimmery strands of translucent plastic and a couple of black eyes. It's eight-thirty in the morning, the tide is coming in, and the bonefish are working their way into the mangroves to eat. When you're lucky, you see them feeding, and as they burrow their noses in the sand for crabs and shrimp, their forked tails come out of the water and flicker in the sunlight like iridescent Japanese fans. A tailing bonefish is the most welcome sight on the flats.

Pap positions us quietly into a place where bonefish will ideally move as the tide comes in. Pap may have been quiet but, like all guides, he becomes animated when he sees a fish. Every angler gets in tune with the sound a guide makes when he first sees a bonefish. A slight whistle, a clicking, or a whispered *okay, okay*. He poles the boat to put the wind at our back.

So after we see a bonefish, here's the plan: I have forty or fifty feet of line ready to cast as soon as Pap gives the word. When I cast, that line can't get tangled, it can't end up under my feet, it can't get wrapped around the reel or around anything else. In the wind this can be hard to do. Then, if you get a bonefish on the line, it can't get tangled on any of these things as it makes its run. The free motion of the line is everything.

Catching a bonefish is hard, so we don't want any of the old human error to cost us the chance at a hard-earned fish. And often it's not until this bonefish is on its run that you realize what a mess the line is at your feet. This is where the trouble starts. Alas, any weakness will be found — a frayed knot, a loop in your line, or some other unimagined obstruction that, like gravity, naturally draws the line toward it, where it becomes entangled just for one second, and in the moment you discover it, the line goes slack. The bonefish is gone.

You return to the well of the boat, slumped and dejected. Now it's your partner's turn. You get to watch him have his time on stage. In that moment of shame you note that the wind has considerably settled down, making his casting easier, that the clouds have cleared, making spotting a fish suddenly easier, almost *impossibly* easy. But you don't mind, no, you don't mind at all.

A lot of nothing can happen in bonefishing. The morning is usually good if the tide comes in and brings shrimp and crab to the flats, and the fish come out of deeper water and start to feed. Finally, Pap speaks. He says calmly: "Eleven o'clock, a school, forty feet." By the time I make out what I was supposed to see, they have closed in and are thirty feet from the boat. I try to focus on dark shadows, they're moving intently. My first cast is too close and the fish dart away. They're a moving target, but I cast *right* at them. Quickly they forgive me, and Pap tells me to cast again slightly to the right. The cast seems too far away, but I'm not taking into account just how fast these fish are moving.

"He sees it," Pap says, energy entering his voice for the first time today, which makes me strip the fly faster, against my better judgment. "He's coming for it." I'm not sure I've paid so much attention to any voice in my life. Pap is behind me and the voice is disembodied. I begin to be disconnected from any observational sense and am wholly dependent on Pap, who could tell me to do anything and I would do it. I've known this man for less than two hours, and I would take his advice about stock futures, who's going to win Wimbledon, a good Volvo mechanic.

I squint and can see a darker, more aggressive movement from one of the shadowy forms. "He's got it!" I feel nothing, no tug, no pressure. I try to set the hook, foolishly, almost heroically idiotically, by raising the rod, which is how to set a fly when fishing for trout. In this case, as I well know, a strip set is required—keeping the rod down, pointed at the water, and pulling line in with your free hand. This is a common mistake for trout stream graduates arriving on the Bahamas for their continuing education. Making a well-known mistake does not diminish the embarrassment.

Luckily my foolish tactics don't submerge the situation. One thing I try to remember is not to sulk so long I miss my next chance, which often comes sooner than expected. In this case it does. Though I pulled the fly away I quickly (if unartfully) slapped it back into the water. And the fish resumed its pursuit of the Gotcha. The hungry bonefish is there again, and this time it takes it so aggressively I can't mess it up. I strip once and feel intense resistance. It's on.

I feel light-headed, as if I'm not responsible for controlling my actions, just witnessing them. I try to prepare for the famous bonefish run. But you can't be prepared for that any more than you can for your first roller coaster drop. The thing I notice is the sound: Zzzzzzzzzzzzzzzzz. The reel fizzes in my hand like it's going to burst into flames, like a power drill but more thrilling. The fly line pulls off in a torrent as the fish streaks away from the boat.

All the bonefish's strength is used at this moment. This visceral connection animates angling excitement, the minutes and hours of quiet and stealth are contrasted with fierce action that brings purpose and proportion to all the downtime. The fly line is gone and there's just backing, the nylon line at the end of the reel reserved for these situations. I reel in as fast as I can. The bonefish obliges and heads toward the boat. It pauses, resists, and suddenly I can reel no more. Then it heads away again, on another run. This time not as long, the fish is beginning to tire. There's another furious reeling session. I can see the vivid gray of its back. One final run and then it's under control. I pull the fish in, and Pap appears suddenly, having silently come down off the poling stand. "Nice," Pap says. "Three, four pounds." I appreciate that he presents the dimensions in a multiple choice format. The bonefish is iridescent, all silver scales, a torpedo with large black eyes. Pap quickly unhooks the fish with a wire tool so he never touches it. It recovers and swims away. Pap smiles for the first time.

The day has officially begun. My adrenaline subsides. I look around at the rest of the flat. The wind is the only sound. I'm a convert. My heart made room for something more.

Within the sport are long traditions, like trout fishing in England and in the rivers and streams around the world where trout came to be found. But using a fly rod to pursue bonefish, and many other saltwater fish, came about more recently. There are books that get into the culture of bonefishing in the Bahamas, *Body of Water* by Chris Dombrowski is a good one. There's also *Tarpon*, a curious and compelling documentary of some of the first fly fishermen to pursue that large, ancient fish on a fly. Directed by Guy de la Valdène, in the loosest sense of the word, it follows anglers in Key West in the 1970s to a jangly guitar soundtrack by Jimmy Buffett (himself a fly expert). There's Tom McGuane, there's Jim Harrison, there's Bill Curtis, the iconic saltwater guide. The gang's all there in Key West. Who knows what they did at night, but in the heat of the day they fished.

They didn't have the luxury of flats boats, which didn't exist in their modern form until the 1990s. They cast from the stern of the boat, their motor raised out of the water, while their friend poles them backward from the bow. They wear cutoffs and have zinc rubbed on their noses (perhaps not the only white substance to get near their nostrils). They use large Hardy reels and fly rods that are much heavier than the fancy lightweight ones we have now. We're not going to get into tarpon here (they can be over a hundred pounds), but watching these men basically invent the sport in front of us is wonderful.

The point is that pursuing a bonefish on a fly rod wasn't inevitable. In many ways, it's a sport in its infancy. The fly angler puts himself at a considerable disadvantage by insisting on using light tackle, which makes it harder to cast into the wind and harder to land a fish. Some people will ask, Why not catch a fish the easiest way possible? Those people are not fly anglers. We foolish idealists don't look for the easiest way, we vote with our hearts. We have a sense of what's sporting, which makes it sound like we might end up in a duel at dawn on the town green. But it's not that. Rather, it's trying to use a set of skills which, when mastered (or at least improved upon), heighten an experience.

The fragility of light tackle brings an intensity to pursuing a bonefish, and, I believe, a symmetry. The angler has something in his favor, the fish has something in *his* favor. And when you put yourself at a disadvantage, you have to get better to do what you're trying to do. Fly fishing, for me and many others, is about identifying skills and improving them. We need to see more clearly, to cast more accurately and efficiently, we develop a more sensitive appreciation of tactics, so we can fight a fish more confidently. It can be humbling when, after years, you finally realize what's at stake.

I returned to Andros a few years later after I had spent more time on the flats. Now I had a better sense of what was what. I was happy to fish again with Pap. I knew more about saltwater guides and their well-formed habits and prejudices. One drives the fastest boat, insists on it, and heads farther out to seek larger fish. Another is more conservative and hopes to increase his luck and intersect with schools of smaller bonefish. Still another loves wading.

It is nice to be back in Pap's company. Now he smiles more easily, he's an incredibly sweet-natured man. You can tell that just by being with him, even when he doesn't speak. Some people, far too few, are like that, their gentle nature unhidden. He opens up slightly. He might tell you that you made a mistake, though only if you asked him. During lunch he disappears on the island where we eat and returns to open his fist. Inside is a handful of large green snails he'll cook that night for dinner. His identity as a gourmand makes sense when we learn that his mother is the cook in the lodge.

Lunch is more relaxing. Pap can take a break from his

work. On the last day of the trip, to my surprise, he asks me a question. He's not one to initiate conversation. "So," he says in his quiet voice. Then he pauses, as if unsure whether to continue. "You write?" Yes, I tell him. "A writer?" he clarifies, as if it's hard to imagine such a thing, like an astronaut or a jockey. Yes, I tell him. "You wrote a book?" He grins then shakes his head. Yes Pap, I say, I have. "No," he laughs. "Too hard." I assure him it isn't. "I couldn't, I couldn't." Now I'm laughing. Why not, Pap? "Too much concentration." Of all the reasons Pap can't write a book concentration is not one of them. The man can focus intensely for hours on end. It's harder to see bonefish than to write a book, I tell him, much harder. Which is true. We're each on the other side of a skill we can never fully understand.

There's no way to explain how to see a bonefish in the wild. Here are a few things that might make it less difficult. But less difficult is still very good. What I learned first is stop trying to see the fish so clearly. This sounds counterintuitive. Aren't we trying to see the fish? Damn right we are! But waiting until you see a fish clearly is usually waiting too long.

So what do we look for?

- *Nervous water.* Or, as they say in Long Island in the Bahamas, where they have a particular accent: *Noyvess* water. This disturbance in the surface comes from a school of fish moving together. Guides can see it, and you can too, often long before you see actual fish.

- *Shadows.* Don't look at the surface of the water, it is said, look through it. Does that make sense in the abstract? Well, it makes sense in practice. You're not seeing the fish, you're seeing their shadows. That is hard, and over time it gets slightly less hard.
- *Scan an area up and down.* If a guide tells you there's a fish sixty feet away at one o'clock, it's harder to spot than you might think. His one o'clock is one thing, yours is another, and sixty feet can be far more elastic than previously thought. Point your rod at what you think is one o'clock and let him tell you if you should move it right or left. Then scan up and down along that line. Hopefully you'll see what he already sees.
- *Start casting.* Don't wait until you see the bonefish to start that process. You'll have to false cast a few times to get the line going and the distance accurate. Do this while you are still looking for fish.

In a perfect world you see the fish, cast to it, and catch it. That's a lot to ask until you've spent a lot of time on the flats. Sometimes you cast to a point and start stripping, according to the word from God (i.e., your guide). No shame there. Your eyes, like so much of fishing, get better when you know what you are doing and work less hard. In the Bahamas heat that is not so easy to do. Who said we were trying to do this the logical way?

• • •

Here's another airport story. Same airport, same pirate, different trip. After landing from New York, we sat on the runway for the usual dubious reasons. I had a connecting flight to Deadman's Cay on Long Island in the outer Bahamas, and it was getting a little prickly. This relaxing trip was already strained, since I had to get my bag, go through customs, check in, and go through security in less than forty-five minutes.

After an excruciating half hour we were released. I dashed off the plane and past the pirate, who said in his normal, non-pirate, voice: "Well here's a man who's been here before." I had fifteen minutes to make the last flight of the day. Could they hold the plane? Calls were being made on my behalf. My big bag wouldn't make it until the next day—I didn't mind, I had my rods with me. Ten minutes later I was rushing through security when a gate agent came forward saying: "Mr. Coggins?" My guardian angel. "That's me," I yelled as I pulled my shoes back on.

The flight had boarded, but they politely kept it at the gate. "I guess there's no time to buy a bottle of rum," I mused lamely. This suggestion was made in the guise of a joke because of its transparent absurdity. I was heading to a rather spartan camp where you brought what you wanted to drink. They offered Kalik beer (a local beer owned by the non-local Heineken corporation) and acceptable white wine (acceptable in the sense that it came in a bottle). If you wanted rum, you brought it, and it was a tradition to buy a good bottle in the airport.

A week on Long Island without rum struck an off note even though I rarely drink rum. When I'm in the Bahamas I'll drink rum, as God intended, like a sailor on leave. "Oh there's time," my guardian angel said, as if a plane full of passengers weren't waiting on the tarmac. I dashed into the duty-free searching frantically for the best aged rum. "What kind are you looking for?" she helpfully asked. There was none of my beloved Rhum agricole from Martinique, but now was not the time to be particular. I found something from Jamaica that was brown (brown is better than clear, in my rum experience), and we went unhurriedly to the gate. We said goodbye, and I walked out, unaccompanied, onto the runway. A young man in an orange security vest sweetly asked "How you been?" and knocked on the door, and the flight attendant lowered the stairway. I got on with my rods, my rum carefully hidden, and that was that. On-time departure was never in doubt.

Heading to Long Island requires planning since this camp is a modest operation. You make your own breakfast, there's no bar, there's no staff to speak of. The owner's cousin drops off dinner. I brought coffee since the other option was instant. I brought rum since the only other option was no rum. There's a balance between something elegant hustled in from the outside—like Elliott Gould's olives for his martinis in *M*A*S*H*—and too much of a good thing. You balance some of what you want while feeling virtuous for living without a few of your favorite things. You're in a remote setting for reason.

Here, on Deadman's Cay, is where I go for bonefishing and to work on my vision. There are miles of flats and wading, often in bare feet, for hours a day. It's the best way to start seeing fish. It might be said that we're hunting bonefish, stalking them. Clyde the guide has a mustache and a slightly hooked nose, he is lean and can walk faster in the water than anybody I've ever met. But mostly he walks slowly, with his eyes in the distance. In a foot of water you don't want to make a sound.

Flats feel different than the ocean, the water is shallow and doesn't get deep for half a mile, longer. You see the ground all the way into the distance and feel a sense of calm. This is one of the world's great landscapes or seascapes or whatever the poets want to name it. It's completely elemental: sand, water, sun, and mild, humid air. Wading hour after hour we become part of it. Walking as silently as we can, always looking.

What are we looking for? Well, Clyde can see signs of fish much farther than I can. His eyes are set in the distance, say two hundred yards, for nervous water, the disturbance in the surface created when bonefish are swimming. He's all angles, like a scarecrow on high alert. He holds his arm away from his body, and his left hand has two fingers together like a hook. I become sensitive to his mood and movements and am aware the second he stops. That's because if he stops it means he thinks he sees a fish. He calls me close to him with his fingers. Together we walk in unison as quietly as possible and position ourselves so, ideally, the fish swim toward us.

On the flats I'm trying to balance a sense of peacefulness and alertness. There's the solitude of being in this landscape, horizontal in every direction. Clyde has gone back to the boat and I am truly unconnected. Only the wind is animated, the sound altering as I turn my head and it pours into my ears. But I can't get too meditative, because I need to be aware of fish. There's a particular frustration among guides when they miss a fish that darts away as we approach. The problem for me is once I think I see a bonefish I start seeing signs of them everywhere, like a British mystery when every character is a murder suspect.

But the bonefish is benign. Large ones swim alone or in pairs. Smaller fish travel in schools for safety. There's an art, whether wading or in a boat, to tacking in a direction so the bonefish swims at you while the wind's at your back, which helps casting a great deal. This implies the bonefish will keep swimming in the same direction, which they often do not, as they are prone to zig and zag for reasons known to themselves. Ideally they are feeding, relaxed and slow. The faster they swim, theoretically, the less likely they are to slow down and take your fly. Though sometimes they do. They might turn again and swim straight away from you. Then there's nothing you can do. You can't cast over their heads—the fly line spooks them. Bonefish have a knack for leaving. There's nothing lonelier than when the guide says, resignation in his voice, "They're going away." Off they go, off the flats in the opposite direction, suddenly perfectly visible. The loneliness is specific and lasting. It feels like they'll never return. Abandoned on the flats, you are alone.

Almost all of the flats off Long Island are just sand. Hardly any coral or weeds—they're lovely and soft enough that you can walk on them barefoot. If we're going over more coral or rocks, then Clyde tells me and I put on rubber scuba diving boots, with a zipper up the side. Even then Clyde still wades barefoot.

Clyde anchors the boat and we set out. He and I walk quietly in warm water. I stand on his left side, as I'm left-handed and have to be ready to cast. I hold the fly in my hand and let forty feet of fly line drag in the water behind me like one long, curved noodle. This is how much I can quickly cast with just one or two false casts. Walking with Clyde feels communal. We are quiet and have the same goal. Each of us has our part: He sees the fish and I try to catch it. I try to see it too, but he sees it first. That's just how it is. He's in deep concentration and I'm also looking hard at the water, though I hesitate to compare what each of us is doing. He's both more sensitive and a better looker.

You depend on the guide, but the guide is invested in you too. When he finally sees a fish, gets you in position, and you mess it up, all his hard work blows away in a gust of your incompetence. He says nothing and doesn't have to. This happens and it's embarrassing. You apologize. You vow it will never happen again. Which is just what you said the last time and no doubt what you will say next time. That's why catching a bonefish is a shared experience. He's working hard and has a stake in what's happening. That's true with guides for other fish too, but there's something satisfying about catching a bonefish when it's a collective triumph.

If we do not see any fish for five or ten minutes after we get to a flat, or haven't seen them for a stretch, Clyde exhales and heads back to the boat. "Walk to that mangrove," he tells me. "Turn left. I'll pick you up on that island." By now the boat is far in the distance behind us, a dash of white against the horizon, it could be a piece of rice. Clyde walks toward the boat and into the sun. I'm alone.

Now I have no other eyes, just mine, and I don't trust them. The flats feel devoid of possibility. There are no fish here, I know it. When they feel empty of life, nothing else seems so empty. It's not like trout fishing when you know they're there but are sulking or disinterested. This is a complete absence. They *could* be anywhere, they *are* anywhere, they may even *be* everywhere, but they're not *here*.

I can't imagine that I'll ever see a fish unless it's tailing. When I spot a shadow that looks like it's moving, then I point my rod at it. If the shadow remains still, stubbornly unmoving off the tip of my rod, I have to accept it's not a bonefish. Bonefish, unless they are feeding, don't stay still. Things that I've mistaken for bonefish: submerged stones and sticks, but also coral, reeds, holes. And animals: turtles, sharks, small fish and rays. Everything starts to look like what I'm desperately trying to see.

I go minutes without seeing a fish, and then I almost walk on top of one. Too close. Good grief. I thought this flat was empty, and out of nowhere there's a fish at my feet. It dashes away. I'm sunk. Of course I was looking in the distance, I didn't imagine one could be closer than that. As if they would only be where I'm gazing. Amateur hour.

Suddenly I see bonefish everywhere, but they're illusions. I keep walking toward the mangrove. The water flows in a small channel between two low islands. I remember that bonefish often patrol these areas since the current brings them food. I start to walk with more confidence. The water is shallow enough that if there's a bonefish I'll see it. And wait, the sun is reflecting off something. It's a tail. It has to be a feeding fish. It *has* to be. When I'm fishing and something good happens, I look around for somebody who isn't there for confirmation. Am I crazy or is that a tailing bonefish?

I don't know what I feel. More than anything I don't want that fish to move. All right. *Stay calm.* I feel alone in the world. I hear nothing. I want to get close enough to make a good cast. But not too close. I try to get in position, afraid he will bolt any moment. The fish is still feeding, unsuspecting, doing bonefish things, living its bonefish life. A close cast will spook the fish.

I think of everything that can go wrong, everything I'm supposed to do and not do. Then I just do what I know how to do. I err on the side of caution, and like an idiot I cast way too far away from the fish. *What the hell!* At least it was far enough away that the fish had no idea what was happening. I cast closer and the tail suddenly disappears. For a second I think it's spooked and it's all over and that I hate the world. Then the shadow turns sharply toward the fly. I don't hurry, and wait until the fish is near the fly, as Clyde always instructs me to do. Then a strip, then another. Its pointy snout follows and turns suddenly, a feeding move. It has the fly. I strip set and feel resistance. A good feeling. One more set for good measure. It's a connection.

The bonefish is on. It heads out to deeper water. Line peels off the reel. Now I can hear. The reel is loud in my ears. This is supposed to be fun, but I feel a mild pang of dread. All I can think is: *Don't botch this*. Its first run is over. I reel furiously. It doesn't want to be in the shallow water and goes on another run but not as far. I reel again and step into the slightly deeper water. I don't have a net (bonefish guides don't use nets and their sports don't either). As it comes closer, it gleams silver in the light. I grab the fly line and pull it toward me. The fish is at my feet, nearly still. Everything is calm. The fight was the anomaly. I pull the shrimp pattern from its little mouth beneath its head. The bottom of the bonefish is smooth and pure white. I set it upright and it gathers itself and speeds to deeper water.

A bonefish. On my own. Not the biggest, but maybe the best. I shake my head and scan the horizon. Clyde is out of sight. I walk over to the island, which is just a strip of reeds a few feet wide. My feet sink in the sand. There's water in every direction and clouds speed low across the sky. The sound of Clyde's motor echoes before I can see his boat, and I wait for him to come around the channel and into view.

PATAGONIA

RAINBOW TROUT

Loss

There's no easy way to get to Patagonia. It's the big one. All the way down. The Southern Hemisphere. An overnight flight, then a two-hour flight (from a different airport), then a drive down a paved road that turns into the longest dirt road you've ever been on. There's no way around that and no way around the romance of Butch Cassidy, Bruce

Chatwin, big skies, and big trout. At night, the stars appear upside down to those of us who live above the Equator. When the Big Dipper is inverted, you know you're far from home.

I dream of places. We all do. For months before a trip, Argentina takes over my imagination. Planning begins months before. Lodges send a list of what to bring, and I analyze it with great interest. I scour eBay and fishing catalogs, plot packing strategies as if I'm about to canoe through the Amazon. As the trip gets closer, I study weather forecasts that will be long out of date when I arrive. I don't care, it feels reassuringly scientific and gives me the illusion of active participation. Then I overreact to these conditions and imagine desolate rain or oppressive heat.

I'll also visit Buenos Aires. I read detailed reviews of steak houses and look forward to seeing the old gaucho tailor on a quiet corner in a remote part of town. I chart a path from one easygoing bar to another, where I'll drink Quilmes beer from frosted mugs, or a glass of sweet vermouth on ice. I find an apartment in a 1920s building with towering palm trees in its courtyard whose roots have upturned the art deco tiles. The duplex is at the top of four steep flights of stairs, decaying the right amount, as if it belongs in a Bertolucci film.

Preparing for the trip, I speculate. I'm possessed with possibilities, I have visions. Wide open spaces and vivid blue rivers electrify my mind. I go to cities for history, for architecture and ambition, to see what humans are capable of. Giotto's frescoes at Santa Croce, the Sanjusangendo temple in Kyoto, the tree-lined paths of the Luxembourg Gardens.

These redefine the limits of achievement, they're humbling and reassuring. I love Florence, Kyoto, Paris. These places make me proud to be a human being. A rare feeling.

When I fish, I forget all that. Patagonia is not what anybody's made, it's what's lasted despite all we've made. This is the natural world at its most direct and I feel lucky to be in a place that's indifferent to me. The sky is high, the landscape varied. Lush and green close to the Andes in the west. Stark, arid, and unrelenting in the east. Patagonia is emptier than most places. Drive thirty minutes any direction from one of the few small cities and it's barely developed. There's a metric for that, people per square mile, or population density. Let's leave math out of it. Why measure what you can feel?

The feeling begins when the flight from Buenos Aires starts its descent into San Martín de los Andes. Out the window is the largest river I've ever seen. The Limay. It's impossibly straight, like a blue highway with no traffic. It's an indisputable fact, a force, something cut through the land an ice age ago. Fools try to dam it and sadly, they've succeeded in places. Better to leave it alone and not try to control it. Better yet, float down it and try to catch a trout.

What strikes me in Patagonia is not just that the water's bluer, though it is, or that the sky's higher, though it feels that way. The land exists on a different scale than we're used to. Not just the size, but the time. If feels wrong to measure time in days or weeks, even years or decades. This goes back to geologic time, beyond memory. Yes, Patagonia gets me worked up.

It's also full of fish. That's another key detail. You'll find wild trout—rainbows, browns, very healthy, living large. Patagonia makes anglers feel like they're going back in time, because there are many trout and few people, the ideal equation. But it's not the past—when I'm here everything feels both present and enduring. I come here to intersect with a landscape charged with the permanence of great places that have nothing to do with humanity. It also gets very specific, wild, and immediate. A flock of parrots flies over the river, a mink runs along the bank, a suspiciously large snake is in the dirt near where we take out the boat. That wildness makes me feel alive.

Patagonia is vast. As in the Louvre, you pick your points. There are many ways to fish here—and they're all great. Get in a drift boat and cast across immense rivers. Wade in brilliantly cold spring creeks. Fish near your estancia and never leave the estate. Hit the road and drive hours to different water every day.

Some highly motivated, possibly insane humans go all the way south, to Tierra del Fuego, where the landscape is lunar, treeless, and the wind breaches fifty miles an hour. If you're talented and lucky, you catch a huge sea-run brown trout, a heroic fish you'll feel compelled to brag about, boring listeners for the rest of your life. It's a gamble, though. If you don't catch that fish, then you'll have the slightly shell-shocked look of a man I once saw in the Buenos Aires airport. He was returning home, shut out, having not done the one thing he traveled four thousand miles to do. That's a long flight to think about what could have been.

• • •

Patagonia is far from civilization and its discontents, but once a day that's not true: Nothing is more civilized than lunch beside a river in Argentina. It's one of life's great pleasures. Lunch with guides in Montana is an afterthought in a paper bag. The guides pick it up at a deli in the morning on the way to meet you at the river. That's fine—you don't need much on the banks of the Madison. Men eat standing up unless they don't even bother leaving the boat. Efficient, without ceremony, the way you'd expect men in the wild to eat. Nothing wrong with that.

They do things differently in Argentina. The first clue is at breakfast at the lodge, which happens, you are told, at eight or nine, and the blessed words: or *whenever you get up*. This is the easygoing Argentinian approach to life. Buenos Aires, after all, is full of restaurants serving dinner to families with young children at 10 p.m. There's none of the military precision that prevails at American lodges, where there can be a competition to see who's awake first. That's a competition I've yet to win, place, or show.

Around two in the afternoon, even three, after a long morning of fishing, the guide pulls the drift boat over to the bank where a previously invisible clearing suddenly appears. He unloads a startling amount of gear that you failed to notice while you focused on fishing. Coolers, dry bags, a gas stove. He unfolds chairs and opens a table, which he sets up and covers with a checked tablecloth. You might think you're moving in for the night. You sit down in the shade of a tree and watch the river. Not trying to catch a trout, you appreciate the surroundings in a less invested way.

The guide takes out a cutting board and starts slicing a garlicky summer sausage and opens a jar of pickled boar (they run in the hills nearby). He cuts up some sharp cheese with a knife that seems slightly too large. He lays it all out and it's impressive. This is the *picada*, the traditional Argentinian board. It makes a lovely lunch.

Then he starts a small propane fire and asks, in a clear escalation of the proceedings, how you like your steak cooked. A bottle of red wine appears, as magically as the clearing did, and is passed around as if it's the most natural thing in the world. A Malbec from Mendoza, in the high-altitude north. And it *is* the most natural thing. Softer, less spicy than the Malbecs I'm used to. It's exceptionally good, and in this place at this time it's about the best thing on earth. On the table is salt, pepper, a local hot sauce only the guides have the courage to try, ripped coarse bread, cold roasted potatoes, a lightly dressed salad. The steak is thin and rare, as is normal here. Nothing is rushed. It's miraculous.

It's so miraculous that you might feel sleepy. That's all right, if you feel a siesta is the best course of action, they've got a hammock they can string between trees. Coffee is needed if you're going to recover and fish. They have that too. Argentinians, in my experience, have a weakness for instant coffee and powdered cream (*creamer*, I guess — a highly upsetting word and concept). Everything is at its own pace. It occurs to me that dinner won't be until 9 or 10 p.m. You pull yourself together and get back on the boat.

The late afternoon remains. There are four more miles to fish. Now, that's a lunch.

How did we get here on the banks of the Limay River on this beautiful blue afternoon? Two friends and I are staying in a handsome lodge near St. Martín. Set on the shore of Lake Lácar, presided over by the gracious mountain Lanín, the small city is one of the centers of recreational life here. It's January, the first month of summer, children are out of school and the highways are dotted with cars heading to camp in national parks, bicycles and tents strapped to roofs.

It's our first morning. Meeting your guide is like meeting your analyst—except you get to choose your analyst. At a lodge the guide is usually arranged for you. Always a charged moment, the sense of anticipation is higher here than usual. Not only will we be fishing with these guides, we'll be camping with them as well. I like Argentinian guides. They're worthy of the old-fashioned term "dashing"—as if they're friends with Francis Mallmann or backcountry skiers, or both.

Enter Boris. He has fair, straight hair, a patchy beard, and is well built, like he played rugby or some other sport where beer was involved before, after, or possibly during. We shake hands, and I get into the passenger seat of his truck, which is attached to a trailer holding a drift boat. We're about to drive over an hour to the put-in. He offers me some yerba maté, the caffeinated drink served in a gourd that's part of the daily ritual here.

Boris, it occurs to me, does not sound Argentinian. This isn't a Paulo or a Diego. Not a Guillermo or a Carlos. Not Spanish from Buenos Aires, not indigenous from the country's interior. Which is to say: a white guy. Not what I was expecting. "Are there many men named Boris in St. Martín?" I ask. "Ah, no." Boris has a mischievous look in his eye. He's Russian. His parents moved here from St. Petersburg when he was young. I'm always curious about what guides do when they're not guiding. In Patagonia, the season is six months, which leaves half the year to be a carpenter, bartender, ski instructor, or whatever else.

"What do you do in the off-season?"

"Mostly just jerk off."

"Only during the off-season?"

"All the time actually."

We've known each other five minutes.

We'll be floating down the immense Limay River with Boris and Peter, our other guide. Another boat, essentially a raft with pontoons, piled high with gear, will go ahead of us while we fish. Two men and a chef will set up a camp where we will all eat dinner and sleep. They'll break it down, float down the river another eight or nine miles, and then set it up again. Three days of fishing, two nights on small islands within the river. A good situation.

The Limay is full of agreeable rainbow trout. There are brown trout as well, but they're harder to find. The rainbow trout is a wonderful fish. It expresses itself and often jumps in the air when hooked. It's not self-aware, like the brown trout. Where the brown trout is wary and resists most efforts to get caught, the rainbow plays along.

Attractive, beloved, maybe not *technically* the most intelligent, though that's never held against them. It's the golden retriever of fish.

Rainbow trout are widely found, and their appearance depends on where they are. They can get downright fat in certain lakes where they eat well and aren't slimmed down by the demands of swimming in the current. Along their top they're a pale, inviting green, covered with small black spots that give way to a brilliant stripe of pink that stands out against their cream stomachs. That all sounds too authoritative. The rainbow trout can have many reflections—they can glimmer silver, the pink becomes deep, almost red. One thing that remains true of all rainbow trout is that their color mirrors the joy of catching one.

On the drive to the river, we listen to wonderful traditional Argentinian folk music, selected by Boris. He confides that it's unusually hot and sunny, and has been for a week. "Can't remember a January like this," he sighs. That's not what you want to hear. Warm water can make fish less active, and the sun makes them less inclined to come to the surface to take dry flies. This makes a philosopher out of you. And I define philosopher in the traditional manner, as somebody who feels guilty he's in a beautiful place but is mad about the weather.

Yes, the trout are down at the bottom, where the water's cooler and they will be safe from osprey and other evildoers. To go after the larger trout, Boris tells us, we will be fishing streamers with sinking lines. He says this with some resignation, since fishing that way is not exactly romantic. You imagine a gracious cast and a small fly rolling out in a poetic loop and a trout coming up to sip it. This is not that. Streamers are large, weighted, indelicate. They look like minnows. You cast downstream at a forty-five-degree angle from the boat, really heave it more than cast it, let the streamer sink and swing with the current, and then strip it in to imitate a darting little fish. A trout chases it and takes it aggressively, leaving you with an electric feeling charged up your arm.

We dutifully cast our streamers down from the boat and let them sink. We do this all morning and catch a few nice rainbows. But the magic is missing. It feels slightly robotic. Finally, we pull over to the bank of an island. Boris has a plan.

We step into the river; we are going to wade. We have to be careful because the water is so clear the rocks on the river-bed look like they're just a few feet down. What appears shallow is in fact five feet deep, even seven. Try to pick one up and fall in over your head, which is known to happen to unsuspecting anglers on this river.

Boris heads downstream with my friend. I'm alone for the first time all day. I wade up the far side of the island. Island might not be the technical term, it's about the size of a good parking space. But the bottom is hard sand and I can stand easily. Across five feet of the Limay is another small island. Between these islands a channel runs shallower and more slowly than the rest of the river. This is where feeding trout will be. The time for speculating is over. It's a perfect holding place for trout to wait out of the current for food to arrive. Trout live simply. They want to expend as little energy as possible, they want to eat and they want not to be eaten. This is a good philosophy of life. I also want to eat without too much exertion, and not be eaten myself. And if I could do that in Patagonia, even better.

The streamers are gone. Now's the time for a dry fly on the surface, time to do this the right way. Well, maybe not the most classical way—there's no hatch to imitate. During a hatch a river is covered in insects, and fish usually eat them aggressively. This is a good thing. Anglers love to tie on flies that imitate what's hatching and drift them over feeding trout. This is what happens on all the fishing trips of our imagination. Rivers full of trout feeding on the surface. If this sounds good to you, then live on a river and head out when a hatch happens. It's hard to predict when that will be while you're choosing your dates in Argentina six months from now. Something happens—a front, a week of rain, another act of God—and you usually arrive a day after an amazing hatch when the guide's grandmother, who'd never cast a fly rod before, caught a 28-inch brown trout on the surface. This isn't what you want to hear. This is why I now ask guides not to tell me about the comically good fishing that happened right before I arrived.

So there's no hatch. But there are other strategies. Most of what trout eat is below the surface—nymphs, scuds, minnows, and more. The fact remains that most anglers, myself included, like to see the fish take the fly on the surface. So we won't go down below if we don't have to. This river has a lot of grasshoppers on its bank that end up on the water, so I tie on a Chubby Chernobyl. Like many great flies it has an awful name. A Chubby Chernobyl resembles a grasshopper in the loosest possible sense. This one has a beige foam body, wrapped to a hook with green thread, with some plastic legs hanging off it. It's topped with a mohawk of white hair (too long in fact—I often give that mohawk a trim). This isn't exactly a noble fly, it looks a little comical, but I can see it clearly and it floats well. These are determining factors when choosing a fly. I want to control it and keep sight of it on the water.

I look up toward the top of the channel. I think I can see noses of rising trout but can't be sure. Is this an angling mirage? That happens to me quite regularly, my desire to see something compromising my optical certitude. I squint. Dark shapes breach the surface, leaving ripples in their aftermath. Yes, they're rising. I know where I want to cast, *the landing spot*, in angling parlance. It's the size of a doormat.

I need to cast the hopper in the channel between the islands and let it float back toward the rising trout. For once, being left-handed is helpful (left-handers are always looking for societal conspiracies designed to counteract our prodigious creative talents). I take my time. The first cast is the best chance, since the trout hasn't seen anything unnatural. This doesn't calm my nerves.

I cast, let the hopper drift, and there's a gentle rise. *Slow take, slow set* is a saying I've repeated many times, since when a trout rises I often get excited, try to set the hook too soon, and pull the fly right out of its mouth. This happens for a few reasons. The first is that there's finally action and you overreact. Another is that we think fast reflexes work best when precision is actually far better. But precision is hard, while speed can be mindless. If a trout comes up slowly (which they're more likely to do in slow water when the fly isn't moving fast), then you have to wait for it to take the fly and head down again. Count a beat. Then, and only then, do you raise the rod and set the hook. Our instinct is to set it as soon as we see the rise. But you just have to wait. It's a leap of faith, and, like any other leap of faith, it's hard.

I say this because there's a rise, a small but clear disturbance in the water where my fly just was. I wait to set the hook, I swear I do, but when I raise the rod, the hopper, unattached to the trout, cannons out of the water and over my head. This is not a good feeling. In fact, it's a bad, bad feeling.

In a few seconds I have gone from

1. thinking I caught a fish, to
2. not catching a fish, to
3. catching the reeds behind me, to
4. swearing that this sport is designed to break me down completely.

After my good-enough cast, the trout and I had not connected.

Missed Connections, Patagonia Edition:

Me: American angler of minor distinction in Argentina.
You: Well-built rainbow trout having a late lunch.

THE OPTIMIST

We just passed each other on the Limay.
Is it me or did we have a moment? Let's do this again.

I exhale meaningfully and look around in as dignified a manner as I can manage, as if everything that just happened was according to some master plan. But I really want to make sure that Boris hasn't witnessed my foolishness. They're downstream dealing with their own angling issues, so I don't have to worry. The only other consolation is that I never felt the fish. If there's resistance, it means the hook briefly pulled in the trout's mouth, and that's that. The trout, understandably confused, will retreat to a safe place and not feed anymore. It's not coming back.

If Boris had been with me, I would have asked if it was my fault—did I raise the rod too soon? Most guides would say I did the right thing. Boris was different. He would say he didn't want to answer, his diplomatic way of saying that yes, I set the hook too fast. Boris wanted to balance being honest with not laying blame but knew that sometimes you can't do both. I was forced to acknowledge that I often think I want honesty when I really want reassurance.

Anglers want to know if whatever terrible situation that's been inflicted upon us is our fault. We want to be absolved of responsibility but also to understand the catastrophe. It's a paradox: We want to learn something without admitting we didn't know it. Fly fishing isn't a crossword puzzle—one correct solution doesn't unlock all the others and make everything fall into place. Sometimes you have to accept not knowing.

It is said that kings are subject to fate, not luck. On a

smaller scale, the angler is master of a kingdom that always threatens to crumble. There are enemies without and dissent within, and uneasy rests his head. His blessing and curse is that he claims all success for himself. By logic, failure would be his alone as well. Since that's unacceptable, he's forced to look around for other causes of fishlessness—conditions, spooky trout, subpar guides, faulty tackle, a lost lucky hat—anything that implicates an outside actor.

We're left to balance cosmic judgment and physics. We tell ourselves we're cursed or chosen, blasphemed or blessed. It's simply too hard to accept that a huge part of the equation doesn't depend on us. That's why we read and study and hoard advice. We want to have as much under our control as we can, but it's never enough. Sometimes it's your fault, sometimes it's not. There's no more reassurance than that, regardless of what the guide tells you. All you can do is make another cast.

So, I'm standing here with my Chubby Chernobyl, whose name has never seemed more ridiculous, deciding how mad to be or not be. At one point in my life, I would have been livid. Casting streamers all morning in the middle of a heat wave, and now I get one good chance on a dry and I miss it. Yes, that's what *might* have gone through my head as a younger man. Now I approach and reject the exit onto Fury Road and let the situation calm down. I let the pool rest, which is hard, because you want to rectify things right away. This time, I'll wait.

Fish begin to rise again. Some seem small (fast, splashy, unconcerned takes of young trout, like teenagers speeding in cars who don't appreciate the inherent dangers of the world). I sense the largest of these fish, in a different class, is on the left. The rise is subtle but deliberate, and moves more water. When a fish like that rises, it makes you pause. The stakes are raised. I can make out its shoulders—yes, fish have shoulders!—the wide area behind the head of a large fish.

That's the fish I missed. It's back. I'm certain. I have another chance and I make one good cast. It floats down the left side of the channel. The Chernobyl disappears beneath the smallest disturbance in the river. But slowly. Slowly, you understand. And, despite all the adrenaline surging down the Limay River and into my left arm, slowly I raise the rod. I wait a beat—and that wait is brutal—and the line goes tight. I feel the weight. It's on.

A large fish takes initiative, and doesn't wait for you to decide what to do. This one swims downstream immediately. I lower the rod tip as it goes. Line peels out. I offer resistance to stop it, if the trout goes too far the power of the current will be with it and I won't be able to turn it back. I race downstream trying not to fall into the deeper water. I call Boris in the most understated way I can, "Hey now!" Boris sprints to the boat to get the net. Why doesn't he have the net with him? Seems like a good question under the circumstances. A really pressing question. A question that allows me to shift the blame for any catastrophe onto somebody else.

It's a superstition, Boris says later. Bring the net, don't catch a fish. Bring the umbrella, it doesn't rain. I know what I think about this superstition, nothing flattering, until Boris is finally standing beside me, net in hand. He doesn't say anything; he knows what I'm trying to do. The fish goes deep enough that my rod tip is in the water. Finally it tires and offers less resistance. I lead it over to the bank and raise my rod and Boris's immense net lifts up a big rainbow. Gleaming silver, deeply pink. A real fish.

"Nice job, buddy," Boris says.

That's the idea. Four thousand miles for a brief moment of triumph. I let the fish go. I let all fish go. This is by rule (many rivers are catch and release) but also principle. I try to keep them in the water, unhook them and return them as quickly as possible. The trout is tired and swims in the shallow water near my boot. In the water, its green back looks dark, the same color as the rocks. If you didn't know it was there, you might miss it. A miracle of evolution. Its tail moves slowly. It's an animal, indifferent to theories, to glory. Those are our ideas. It finally swims off. The thrill recedes, replaced by a fleeting sense of shame that I cared so much in the first place.

We pull off the river after 8 p.m. The sun begins to set, the light softens, and the heat of the day finally subsides. The river turns dark, still as a mirror. The last light is a thin sliver over the bluff. Boris pulls the boat around a bank and suddenly the camp, which had been hidden behind trees, is illuminated, in full view.

In the clearing, the camp glows under the dark sky, like a stage set. A series of spotlights shines on a small bar and a large table, set for dinner. Beyond it, in a large military mess tent preparations have already begun. There's a fire with a small iron grate grilling chorizo, the traditional sausage Argentines often have to start a meal. Tato, the chef, is in his element. We learn later that he was a skier with professional ambitions. He has vivid eyes and a combustible disposition. Two other men are responsible for clearing the site, setting up and breaking down camp, which, we now realize, is serious work. This is no ordinary camp.

Paco, one of the camp masters, shows us around. "Come," he says. He opens our tents, set in a row along a trail in the back. He demonstrates how to use the sink and shower, how to start the hot water, everything has been considered. This well-planned camp feels like it's been here forever, not four hours. There's even a makeshift toilet I don't want to recall in too much detail.

I rinse off. There's a mirror hanging above the sink, I comb my hair, like I'm ready for a night in Buenos Aires. After my fishing clothes, my clean shirt feels very clean. If I had some Old Spice, I would put it on. I make the best gin martini I've ever had in my life. This is how camping should be! With lights, running water, a bar, and, crucially, set up by someone else. Sitting by the fire as the sun sets with no signs of life anywhere is a wondrous feeling.

After dinner, we toast the chef. I pour Tato some old Cuban rum I brought, and we raise our glasses. It's not clear who among us is least sober, the competition is considerable. Boris and Peter depart early to their beds, exhausted. Tato and the others will sleep on cots in the mess. They stay up late, cigarette smoke and laughter floating toward our tents. We can hear their voices in the distance when we finally fall asleep. The next day they'll break it all down, stack everything high into their raft, and float past us down the river.

I wake at 4 a.m. The voices are gone. Everybody's asleep. I go outside. The stars are spread across the entire sky like the sea. The most I've ever seen. We're far from everything on this little island in the middle of the wide river. Unconnected from land, from everybody who knows us, from everything happening in the world. We are elsewhere. But we aren't elsewhere, we're here. And it feels better that way.

I return to Patagonia on a different trip, to the same small airport in San Martín. I'm greeted by a tall man with a strong, dark brow and a wise-looking smaller man. They're both in the well-worn khaki clothes often found on anglers. They nod at me. I'm wearing something similar beneath an old, drab sport coat. We get into their truck, and Nestor, the taller of the two, drives us to the lodge. It's a surprisingly short drive by Patagonia standards—less than two hours, and, remarkably, no dirt road. "Older anglers appreciate no dirt," the wise man says. This is Jorge.

Nestor stops the truck in front of an imposing log building with a stone chimney. We're greeted by our hostess, a smiling, dark-haired woman from Colorado. She manages the lodge with her husband, who does the cooking. She offers us a tray of empanadas, still warm, and a glass of red wine. Now this is a welcome. Standing beside her is the small staff of the lodge and we are all introduced. My love of Argentina is undiminished.

The next morning, Jorge and I fish the Collón Curá. Nestor, who's the lead guide, rows. I fish from the front. Jorge, a pioneer of Patagonia fly fishing, is in the stern. He's one of the original outfitters who's brought American anglers to Patagonia for decades. He's fought successfully to keep dams from being built in the great rivers, sometimes unsuccessfully (there are still unfortunate dams in the area—they have the same problems as the US, alas). I don't fish with somebody like Jorge very often.

Nestor pushes the boat off. The Collón Curá is wide and unhurried. Nestor does the heavy lifting. Tall, earnest, expert, he makes sure everything works. He's quiet, highly capable, and I trust him immediately.

We're on the water. It's time to fish. From the back of the boat, Jorge hums "Wish You Were Here," and speaks with great appreciation of Pink Floyd, something I had not counted on. I'm excited. I cast a fair distance, trying, I suppose, to make a good impression. Jorge watches me politely, with mild interest, even bemusement. Why cast so far? his look seems to ask. There's good water near the boat. In this river, there's good water everywhere. Jorge proceeds to cast about fifteen feet away, well within the length of casts I just made. He catches three rainbow trout in about ten minutes.

He fights these fish patiently, with a sense of assurance. I've never seen rainbow trout like this. They're sleek and silver and so strong. They don't have the vivid color of rainbows I've known, but are streamlined, silver slabs. Unlike most rainbows, who are reluctant fighters, these won't come to the boat. They go on run after run. Jorge takes his time landing them and laughs to himself, amused at some combination of the ease and agreeability of these fish and his own secret knowledge. Possibly he's amused at my approach. Like other expert anglers I've known, Jorge resorts to complicated maneuvers only when he has to. He does simple things simply. If he has to double haul into the wind he certainly can. If he has to make an elaborate mend—throwing out line so the current doesn't drag the line, and the fly appears natural to the fish—then, and only then, does he do so. He doesn't have time to show off, he's busy catching fish.

Jorge understands how to catch fish in the middle of this river, one he knows well. I struggle, looking for a target—a rock or a bank. Later in the morning, the river narrows and we approach a bluff. The current forms an eddy behind a projected rock, a small, protected space next to the bank—a perfect holding place for a good fish. I have time to make an accurate cast to that calm water. Then I'll have to throw out more line, a mend, to keep the fly from dragging. I make the cast and toss in a mend. The fly sits there. No fish. I throw another mend. It still sits there waiting. No take from one of the supposedly agreeable rainbows. I have half a second before the fly will drag and still no fish will take it. But it's such a good spot—there has to be a fish there. Still, the hopper sits there dumbly. I'll have to pick it up to make another cast.

At the last possible moment the calm water is pierced by the decisive rise of a big rainbow. It might have been near the bottom and finally decided to come to the surface for the hopper. "Yes!" Jorge exclaims. He's been watching carefully and appreciates the situation. I've seen how Jorge takes his time landing trout and now I imitate that. It's my first really good fish of the day and I can't believe its strength. It fights harder than any rainbow I've encountered. This fish pulls down, insistently. It keeps pulling out line, I keep reeling in, then it goes on another run. It's almost like the smallmouth bass in Wisconsin. Finally I bring it to the boat and Nestor calmly nets it. These trout are in a different class, truly wild fish, worthy of the river. I'm exhilarated but try to hide my excitement. I just smile at Nestor. He smiles back.

Here's how this story ends in Patagonia. It's simple, really. Endings bring clarity, for better or worse. It was the last day, the last stream. It would be another year before I would return to Patagonia. Even that would require luck. We'd been on big water, we'd done well. We thought we'd take a chance on a spring creek for a large trout. The chances were long, but that was all right. Jorge knew the perfect place.

After a hairy drive down a rarely used dirt road, we park and hike into a creek not often fished. It's always exciting to come to new water. It's full of possibility. We walk down a path and stand on a high bank, the stream is twenty feet below. It's a sunny day, the water clear, the trout skittish. Beneath us is a deep pool, the trout are so large they look like slow-moving logs. These are true predators that feed at night, on smaller fish, even on mice. They lay low in the day at the bottom of deep pools. In this light, they're nearly impossible to catch.

We continue down the stream until it becomes shallower. It's too high to cast down to the fish, and there are branches and brush between the bank and the water, anyway. It's decided that I'll climb down into the water, while Nestor and Jorge walk ahead along the ridge and look for trout. They'll tell me when they see a trout and I'll cast to it. This stalking method is used in New Zealand, a place I've never been. I know it's high risk, rare reward.

No accommodation has been made for the angler—there are no paths down to the water, no brush has been removed along the banks to facilitate casting. Getting into the water is no easy feat. It's a brambly situation. The water, I can't help but notice, is very cold. The Lanín peak sits in the distance, faintly covered in snow.

Walking in a freezing stream waiting for somebody else to find a trout is a new experience for me. To an observer, I might resemble a biblical figure, sentenced to wade the world's waters atoning for a grave sin. I'm a passive participant in this strange equation. I gaze up, expectantly, at Jorge and Nestor. They are my eyes now, but I feel their eyes on me, like I'm on stage. This is intensified because what I have to do is exacting. When they see a trout, I'll move as close as I can, forty feet below it, and try to make one good cast to where the fish lies. The trout will take the fly or be spooked and retreat. I'll have one shot.

I wore waders every day of the trip, but we were in the boat and ended up wading very little. So I wet-waded today—I just wore chinos—and that was my first mistake. Spring creeks are often small and easy to fish from the bank or from shallow water. This is not like that. I'm in the middle of a wide stream in frigid water up to the place where I can feel it most. I try to concentrate on other matters.

Just when I'm starting to wonder if this whole production is a ridiculous gambit, Nestor snaps me to attention. "David," he says intently, moving slowly along the bank. He's so thin, he looks like a mannequin as he gets on his knees so he won't disturb the fish. "Large brown, feeding," he stage-whispers. "Behind the tree." Jorge moves up behind him to observe. This is an impressive audience for what I'm about to attempt.

I follow his gaze along the far bank. I can see the sunken tree in the water but not the trout itself. I know where I have to cast. I remain as far away as possible while still giving myself a chance. I'll make one false cast, parallel to Nestor's side of the stream, then let go the full cast at an angle across to where the fish is holding. I can't keep false casting, because the shadow of the line will make the trout bolt. I have on a large hopper which, *in theory*, should entice a larger fish to come to the surface.

There's a small window, and I mean small, behind the tree in front of the fish. This is hard, but I want it to be hard. In fact, it's extremely hard, so maybe I want it to be slightly less hard. This is supposed to be fun, right? It's many things, but I'm not sure it's fun. I try to relax. I've dreamt about this place all year. I exhale. *I can do this.* I've been preparing for this moment. One false cast, I add a second one, the line speed is correct. This is my chance, this is my moment. I release the cast. And it's . . . short. Just. Slightly. Short. Short is the word for it. Ask one hundred people and they would all describe the cast as short. They might not be anglers, they might be new to such things, but they would know the cast was short. The fly lands right on top of the trout's head.

The fact that the cast is on line is no consolation. Accuracy in this situation requires correct distance. The fish spooks, of course. I can tell because even from this distance I can see Nestor and Jorge wince. I wanted to catch one last trout and they wanted me to, as well. I was so close! I'm disappointed in myself, and, I'm afraid to say, I suspect they're disappointed in me, which is almost worse.

"Wait!" Nestor interrupts the demoralized atmosphere. "Another fish is there." It's a good lie. A feeding fish will install itself in the best lie, like the banquette in its favorite restaurant. If it vacates the slot, then another fish might slide in to take it. That's just what happened. "A rainbow," Nestor says. "A good one." From his tone, and sense of urgency, I know he means it. The rainbows here are immense. Now I have my distance down correctly. I pull two more feet of line from the reel: I will not be short this time. With the pressure off—I've already disappointed everybody—I drop a very respectable cast right where I want to. It will drift down to the waiting rainbow.

As soon as the hopper lands, the water erupts. It looks like an anvil dropped onto the stream. But *in front of the fly*, not behind it where the rainbow is. From its new hidden holding place under the tree the brown trout has *launched* itself at the fly. Nestor can't contain himself. "It's the brown," he says. Louder now: "It's the brown!"

Nestor's shocked. Jorge springs to his feet. He's shocked. My eyes have never been wider. I'm shocked. The brown

127

destroys the hopper. It's a truly large fish. Despite everything I've said about emotional anglers, you have to believe me when I say that it's the biggest brown trout I've ever had on my line. Well over two feet. Seriously, I wouldn't lie! The fish electrifies the rod, I feel a shot in my arm. I'm connected with something truly wild.

An unequivocal fact of fishing is that once you do one thing well you will be tested some other way. The drama of the cast was over now. That was act one. It was a good cast and now it's time to forget about it. If all you want is to make a good cast, then do it in your backyard. You're on the water for a reason—now land the trout, man!

There's barely a current, which is to my advantage. The trout quickly goes deep. I'm ready. I have it under control for about half a second, possibly three-quarters of a second, but definitely less than one full second. The trout changes tactics and comes downstream toward me. Again, I'm prepared, and quickly reel in line. I feel a faint hint of satisfaction. That satisfaction soon vanishes. This is as far as I've planned. Like a bank robber who hasn't thought out the getaway, I have the diamonds and no escape route. The fish goes directly for the far bank, which I now realize, to my horror, is lined with submerged branches. I saw them before, but then they seemed abstract. Now they're very real. This is the last place you want a large fish on a fine tippet to go.

I assess this delicate situation. I can pressure him and keep him out of the bushes, but not too much or he'll break off. Or I can let him run, but not too much or he'll go into those branches and nose off the fly. Be too aggressive or be too safe? I have to make a decision. I know I don't want to break him off. And I don't. I don't force him. He goes under the bank, just a bit, before I stop the line. But a bit turns out to be too far. The hopper quickly comes shooting out, and my rod, a moment ago bent, deeply pressured by a huge trout, now is flat, useless as an old lottery ticket. It's over as quickly as it began. The finality of a lost fish, glory replaced by a startling, sudden exclamation of failure.

It's finished. The air hasn't changed, but the day is transformed. The water suddenly feels violently cold. Later, Jorge would say I shouldn't have let the fish go under the bank regardless of the threat of breaking him off. "Keep him away from the bank," Jorge said in a tone meant to be remembered. "You can't let them go in there." I've lost fish and forgotten them. Or learned something from them or tried to be a better person or some nonsense like that.

A few haunt your memory. Later, I'd try to make sense of it. If you admit something matters to you, then when it shatters has to matter as well. There was a lesson in there somewhere, but I didn't know where. It hadn't arrived. There's a time when what unfolds can't be soothed with conciliatory words, or laughed away. The moment for talking would come later. The walk back along the stream was quiet. The mountain still loomed in the distance. We all knew what had happened. The last fish, on the last day. The trout for a thousand stories, a fish for all time. No, nobody said anything about that. They didn't have to.

That night, the chef at the lodge, Julio, a young man with a dark beard, makes a final dinner. It's the *asado*, the traditional grill, cooked over an immense fire. In the face of a terrific meal, matters regain their proper perspective. The Malbec also helps. I'm grateful to Jorge and Nestor, for all their kindness and expertise. After a long day, and a little more Pink Floyd, they're off to bed.

Now I'm alone. I head outside and sit by the fire. The lodge is set on a bluff just above the river. It's a clear night and stars are everywhere. Everything is magnified in Patagonia, it exists on a heroic scale. Without distractions the pleasures here are more vivid, more elemental. I'm leaving the next morning. Patagonia is so far away in every sense—is that why I feel the departure more intensely than usual? If I feel more alive here, then what does it mean to return to life on more modest terms? I let the fire go out and head up to my room. Through the open window I can still hear the river below.

NEW YORK

STRIPED BASS

Intuition

The Waverly Diner on Sixth Avenue in Greenwich Village is open twenty-four hours, every day of the year, even Christmas. I have very warm feelings for this diner, but it's about the last place you want to be on Christmas, a close second to a bus station. About fifteen years ago, I was having dinner at the Waverly when I realized I'd eaten every meal of the day there, which was neither reassuring nor that upsetting. I lived around the corner on Washington Place and was in an unmotivated phase of my life. I spent less time cooking and more time at Film Forum matinees and writing for magazines that are now out of business.

That was before they renovated the place, a decision which satisfied nobody. Instead of feeling pleasantly stuck in a 1950s time warp which was accepted, agreeable, and familiar, the Waverly was updated and felt stuck in a 1970s time warp. They changed décor; I changed apartments. Even though I still live a few blocks away, I stopped going after the makeover—only if I was hungover and wanted a fried egg on a roll, which is a very specific feeling.

Recently, though, I've started to return more often. I'll go at 6 a.m. on a Saturday, one of the rare times the Waverly is empty. No NYU students, no old-timers getting revved up on a Paul Krugman op-ed, no young tourists who've closed down MacDougal Street bars and haven't gone back to their obscure Midtown hotels. Nobody. The streets are empty too. I wait by the cash register with its ancient bowl of powdery mints until breakfast is ready. It doesn't take long.

It's still dark as I take a cab down to the Wall Street Ferry beneath the Brooklyn Bridge. The ferry is well run and always on time. This is the first one of the day, and I take it to Breezy Point in the Rockaways. The city feels shy at this hour, like it's just waking up and hasn't had coffee yet.

I'm going to meet Joel and we're going to try to catch a striped bass. Rumors of stripers arrive in New York before the fish do. There's talk, with the whispered intensity of an inside tip at a racetrack, about the migration. This is passed along among anglers like insider information, and speculation mounts. You don't know how many people care about striped bass until you mention you're fishing for them. Everybody has a source, a friend a hundred miles south who says they should be up your way in a few days. My barber, who's from Long Island, casts from the shore of his house out there, and he tells me as soon as he starts seeing stripers.

This happens in May, when they come up the Atlantic coast to spawn. Stripers have done this since at least the 1600s, when settlers noted their arrival and tried to catch them. In Maryland, where they're the state fish, they're often called rockfish, which lacks a certain dignity that the striped bass has earned. In the fall, when the water cools down, they head back to their home in the South.

Striped bass come in many sizes. There are *schoolies*, the undergraduates of the striped bass world, less than sixteen inches, which are thrown back. There's a good-size fish, eighteen to twenty-eight inches, which can legally be kept, called, naturally enough, *keepers*. There are huge fish that people pose with for photos and insist on telling you about. These can be twenty pounds, or even more; they've enjoyed full lives, and can be thirty years old.

A striped bass is not technically a bass. It's not related to the smallmouth bass we used to catch in Wisconsin. You've seen a striped bass and probably eaten one. It's a block of silver and white, with a swish of black down its side. A striped bass is an athletic, even a social fish. It swims with its colleagues, who are more like friends, it doesn't have too many hang-ups or obsess over its own mythology, like trout do. It's got places to go. It resides in salt water but migrates north along the Atlantic coast to spawn in freshwater. Along the way, striped bass stay in the shallows, relatively close to shore, so they're easily found by the people who want to catch them. They also feed aggressively, which naturally endears them to anglers. The striped bass is a well-loved fish, among poets and populists alike.

Subcultures usually meet in secret, at clubs for obscure bands, at temporary art galleries. Large ones meet in convention centers and dress up as comic book characters. In New York, people are forced to practice their passions wherever they can. Ballet classes in a West Village apartment, soccer leagues on a Hudson River pier. Life drawing classes, rowing clubs, sake societies, listening parties for Wagnerians—New Yorkers will always find their fellow travelers.

In Jamaica Bay, the subculture is right out in the open. People who love to fish make their way to the water any way they can. They cast from rocky points, sit in kayaks and dubious rowboats. They stand on bridges, their lines hanging fifty feet down to the water below. They wade off beaches, they charter large boats or rent small ones. You can't believe how many people fish in New York until you head out to the Rockaways on a Saturday afternoon.

I sit on the roof of the ferry. The first time I did this it felt like I was getting away with something. You can just take a ferry in New York? In theory I knew this existed, in practice it feels too fun for New York. New York amusement is usually related to museums and bars, street life and theater, to culture. Even Central Park feels very much of the city. The ferry feels like a release, easy and unconcerned. Maybe that's why everybody on it looks so happy.

The first stop is Red Hook, where couples go to Ikea and argue over what their apartment does or does not need. Then it pulls away and suddenly we're in more open water. It's easy to forget just how much happens on the water near New York City. We pass immense, garish cruise ships, sleepy barges slowly moving their cargo, large sailboats, the Statue of Liberty. The ferry goes under the Verrazano-Narrows Bridge, which connects Staten Island and Brooklyn. The skyline starts to recede behind us, but the city already feels far away. You might make out a seal or even a whale. Now we're in Gravesend Bay and turn east. Brighton Beach is on our left, the Coney Island cyclone slumbering on the shore.

It's a good place to eat breakfast, so I take out my fried egg on a roll. I feel that familiar sense of reassurance of recovery, of self-improvement. In less than an hour the boat lands at Breezy Point. Joel waits next to his truck. This is early for me, but Joel is up before sunrise most days. Understated and considered, Joel fishes in a methodical way, taking his time and doing things correctly. You would trust his advice, which he offers only when asked. He restored a Boston Whaler, which is what we're fishing in today. Joel has many virtues. At the risk of sounding materialistic, owning a boat has to be considered a virtue as well.

We drive to the marina, another subculture. The parking lot is full of trucks and boats on cinder blocks waiting to be repaired. It's a little neglected. It looks like the final scene in a 1980s action movie where the cops catch the villain trying to get away in a forklift. Incidentally, a lot of retired cops keep their boats here. There's a small building, painted simply with a fish mural on a tropical green background. After a day on the water, members of the marina drink on the deck and talk about the fishing, sometimes they cook out. It's very unpretentious. Joel is one of two people who keep a boat here who fly fish, which places us a little on the delicate side of things. Like playing a Simon & Garfunkel song on a biker bar's jukebox.

We load rods, fill the cooler, stow our dry bags. Seagulls shriek, looking for food. The dull, insistent smell of dead fish hangs in the air. A tail fin, possibly from a shark, is nailed to the wooden post of the dock. The air is still brisk, but now the sun is up. Joel pulls us slowly out of the marina and we pick up speed as we enter Jamaica Bay.

The water is calm. Jamaica Bay is protected on its southern edge by the thin peninsula of the Rockaways. The north side, the bay itself, is curved, where Brooklyn meets Queens. You can tell where Queens begins because that's where the JFK runways are. They're hard to miss. You might have looked out of a plane at JFK and seen water—that's Jamaica Bay. Once, we were about to take off on a bonefish trip to the Bahamas and we could see people fishing out the window. Markley found a photo a guide had just posted of a huge striped bass. We wondered why we were going so far away when there were fish right here. The answer, of course, didn't involve logic.

In the middle of this watery expanse is the Jamaica Bay Wildlife Refuge, a series of small islands and saltwater marshes, with sea grasses and horseshoe crabs and turtles. There are shorebirds, many of whom stop here along their migration. It's the rare landscape that's reminiscent of what was here when the Dutch ran the city four hundred years ago. It's easy to forget that New York was attractive to settlers for its position on the water. The finance center, Broadway, the museums, the penthouses—that all came later. In the beginning, New York was a maritime city. It still surprises me to remember that.

New Yorkers ate fish from Jamaica Bay, and oysters too, until World War I, when the water became too polluted. Environmentalists have worked to clean it up, and I feel lucky to be in what's technically the city's largest open space, with any of the three hundred species of birds that pass through. Thankfully, we've never encountered any dead bodies, which have been known to turn up here from time to time.

It's late September. I associate striper fishing with the arrival of fall. You can chase them early in summer, but that's when I'm occupied with trout. I like the fall tradition of striper fishing, it's set in the calendar. The days get shorter and you appreciate some of the last fishing of the year. It's a glorious New York day and we're not alone. There are already boats about. An hour later everybody who can get on the water will be on the water. People in kayaks tied to bridges, professional boats fishing six rods, even the occasional hotshot fly guide and his sports. Spin casters are on every projection and every boardwalk testing their luck with the same long-shot belief that they'll win the exacta. Against all this are pale green reeds drifting in the wind, stark white egrets taking their time as they wade, their thin long legs like pairs of chopsticks.

The A train runs in the distance on a strip of track that connects the Rockaways to the city. For a minute it seems peaceful, but wait, above us a jet takes off from JFK. On Runway Four, immense Airbus 380s line up before heading to Morocco, South Africa, Japan. They rise in silence at precise intervals, and their sound catches up with us as they climb, and continues after they disappear out of sight. Then it's quiet again, the modern world disappears, and the natural world asserts itself until the next plane takes off.

Trout fishing can be technical, delicate, and a lot can go wrong. Striper fishing is less fraught and more muscular. The rods are heavier, the flies larger, the leaders stronger. You won't get tangled or caught in trees—there are no trees. Trout fishing requires a constant state of balance, stillness, and assurance. It's rarely about force. Fly fishing for stripers is different. The leader won't break off, so you can fight a fish aggressively. This isn't bad—it's liberating. You don't have to worry about the presentation of your fly, which is usually a streamer, you just need to get it out there and retrieve it rapidly.

None of this is a criticism (which, of course, makes it

sound like criticism). It's fun. You're in the open. Let in the sunlight and enjoy it. This is not quiet and considered. In Jamaica Bay it's all happening. This isn't a hushed play, it's a Broadway musical. This isn't the chess club, it's a campus-wide party. Come as you are. Striper fishing is about opportunism, intuition, and luck.

We use Clouser Minnows, one of the enduring fly patterns and perhaps the most well used. The Clouser is a work of art in the sense that a Bic lighter is a work of art: simple, useful, essential—a weighted hook and some bucktail and a few strands of a reflective mylar that flickers in the water. The Clouser comes in many colors and sizes. It darts through the water and shimmers in the light like a baitfish. If you can invent a better imitation of a minnow than Bob Clouser did, then you will be a legend too.

We look for gulls that congregate over schools of baitfish and plunge down into the water and try to eat them. The striped bass have the same idea. They're below the baitfish and crash through the surface of the water trying to eat them too. We want to enter ourselves into this equation. Everybody wants to profit from the misery of the poor baitfish. "Baitfish" is a general term for bunker, herring, mackerel, anchovies, sculpins, and other fish that swim in large schools. The ones we imitate are about three inches long.

The striped bass have moved into the bay, at least that's our hope. We want to intersect with them while they're feeding on the baitfish that are busy living their baitfish lives in the Tri-State Area. Joel steers the boat over to some diving gulls and cuts the motor. We cast toward the mayhem and strip in as fast as we can. Floating closer, we look for bass feeding on the surface. This isn't the subtle rise of a trout. It's a miniature explosion, like a firecracker going off, or a plate falling in the water.

We're hoping to see a shocking streak of white emerge from the dark water and hammer the Clouser. It always strikes me how fast they are. If you connect, you get to fight a strong saltwater fish with tackle heavy enough that it can't break off. The rush of the jets sounds like applause from the gods at your angling genius.

That's the theory, anyway. Anglers are given to hunches and contrary opinions; we have a weakness for going our own way against popular belief. Nowhere is this more evident than striper fishing. A trout angler can pursue the sport in private, which is part of its immense charm, like a meal you prepare for yourself. The stakes, such as they are, are known to you alone. Striper fishing is a very public and moveable feast.

That's because you're in contact with other boats, including well-equipped ones run by professional fishermen. They have depth finders and radars that tell them where there are signs of life, where the fish are. This isn't just a sport, it's their livelihood. When you see this well-equipped boat, do you follow it? You could. Do they know something you don't know? Hell yes! They have a computer telling them what to think. Is that different than following the gulls? I'm not sure. Do you forgo this madness and instead go to a secret place? Or do you follow a well-known guide's boat and see what he's telling his sports to do? This isn't solitaire. It's more like craps if everybody had their own set of dice.

The challenge is maintaining conviction and perseverance. Once you settle on something, don't deviate from it. At least until you've spent an hour catching nothing. There are other variables—there are always more variables. Which fly to use, the speed and rhythm of the retrieve. Also patience and the big knack. You're not just thinking about the fish here, you're dealing with other boats. That's just part of striper fishing in New York. There are six or eight or even twelve other boats in the area trying to do the same things you're doing. Often very close at hand—less than a hundred feet away, motors running. The issue becomes logistical. You physically have to be in position to cast (ideally with the wind at your back). And if a boat arrives at high speed (which happens quite a bit), the stripers will stop feeding and quickly go down.

When fish are rising, there are eruptions all around you. Stripers streak across the water in a white flash, seemingly out of nowhere. They're fast and feed aggressively, they don't bother with the particulars. You're not obsessing over presentation here, just get the damn thing out in the water and bring it in at high speed. But there are still strategies and, more than that, feelings that good striper anglers possess. There's the same sixth sense that expert gamblers have and you start to appreciate it when you realize that you don't have it.

When gulls start feeding, there's a mass movement of boats toward them, all in the hope that the stripers will be there. Motoring at high speed with all the other boats feels slightly anarchic. Sometimes the gulls will sit down on the water just as you arrive. It's over. Then another group starts feeding somewhere else. It's off to the races again. This sense of chaos is like the paparazzi chasing after Marcello Mastroianni on a Vespa in *La Dolce Vita*. Unfortunately, we're the paparazzi, not Marcello.

Despite the mayhem of the boats, striper fishing is more relaxed and open than any other fishing I do. So much of trout fishing is stealthy. It takes place on a river or stream with clear boundaries and parameters. Bonefishing is stalking and silent. What's liberating and joyful about saltwater fishing and striper fishing in particular is the sheer wide-openness of the sport. We're in a boat and can go wherever we want to go. The possibilities are endless. That is enough.

There's a way to make this more complicated, but why do that? Well, we know why—certain anglers won't keep things simple. That's their nature. That's the enduring distinction between Carter's obsessive, evolving tactics and Dave's rigid, consistent ones. But some factors improve striper odds, and anglers like Joel take an advanced approach. Joel is on the faculty of an art school in Greenwich Village. In his fishing hat, he looks like he could be a relief pitcher in an old baseball film. Joel studies and plans. He ties his own flies, knows migratory patterns, lunar cycles, and consults tidal charts.

Every time we fish together, I learn something from Joel—the names of specific baitfish or different channels where bass gather. Like many anglers, he accesses a network of information—books, websites, wise friends—that he refers to in private and only shares when needed. Like a good guide, he knows where baitfish should be and where stripers might follow. That's why well-known fly guides charge huge fees and people will pay them. Suddenly striper fishing doesn't seem so haphazard anymore. I should know this from my time with Carter, but I keep learning that nothing is as simple as it seems.

That doesn't mean we always succeed. The stripers can be in the area but not come into the bay to feed. Joel and I had a bad day once and were sure there were no fish around. It was easy to think that, and who could blame us? There were no birds, no rises, no signs of life. We caught a few small ones, accepted that, and felt fine about ourselves. That night Joel sent me an Instagram photo taken by a guide we'd seen that day. His sport was holding an enormous striped bass, worthy of being mounted. Suddenly our day seemed a lot more modest, but we told ourselves we didn't mind.

Fishing can be solitary, there's the joy of catching a trout in private—and it's a serious joy. Fishing with a friend is different. A partnership begins the second you step into the boat with another person. Now your goals are aligned. I fish with people I like, and I'm lucky to have good angling friends in my life. But I would fish with somebody I barely knew if they were serious about it. I don't have to have much in common with them except their enthusiasm. If it's intense, that's enough.

When I started fishing with Dave and Carter, that was all I knew. They were my grandfather's age and were friends of his. There was a formality to our interactions. Fishing was how we expressed our personalities. That's where obsession and intensity came into relief. Carter could be happy for me because I made a cast that he knew was hard for me. Dave and I could look at a bank and think the same thing at the same time. He'd be the one to say what we were thinking since he did most of the talking.

It was different as I got older and made my own friends who fished. These people lived in New York, were my own age. I remember how I started fishing with Joel. I was standing outside the Quad Cinema on 13th Street one afternoon. Joel walked by on his way to teach. We hadn't seen each other in years, though we knew we were fellow angling travelers. As we were catching up, Joel mentioned he had a boat and was going fishing that weekend. I told him not to tease me, that I was free this weekend and that I didn't turn down fishing invitations. He said he was serious and would never joke about something as serious as that. We met a few days later. The intervening years washed away. Being on the water was what mattered.

Joel doesn't talk as much as Dave, that's for sure. I can fish with many personalities. What counts is a shared set of values. You try to catch some fish at a good but relaxed pace. You want to remember there's more to the day than catching fish. Fishing with somebody else forces you to honestly assess what you care about. Essentially: how intensely to fish and how much action you need. It's also important to have a generosity of spirit—you want each other to succeed. The boat does well together or struggles together.

Angling with a friend intensifies that friendship. You might triumph or struggle, but you'll know each other better. Some friends make sense for certain types of fishing and others for another. The same way you'll see an Ingmar Bergman film with a friend who's into Scandinavian angst and *Heat* with a friend into hard-boiled, Los Angeles crime. If I'm with my friend Matt, who requires action, we're not going salmon fishing. Before I cast judgment on Matt, it's worth remembering that I'm not the right companion for certain fishing either. Markley loves to hike into a mountain stream to catch native eight-inch trout. That's well and good, but I'll be fine down here where the big fish are.

Once established, angling can support the weight of a friendship at a great distance. I'll head out to Idaho to see my friend Taite, a guide in Ketchum. He takes me to some secret places, and kindly helps me catch a few lovely cutthroat trout. Then, when I've caught what seems like enough for a visiting New Yorker, he starts to catch much larger fish out of water I can't reach. He always gives me first shot. Then, in as polite a way as he can, he shows me what's really possible. Taite's beautiful casting and incredible drifts down Silver Creek seem to say, "With another decade of practice, you can do this too." This all happens in the spirit of friendship, and, like Dave and Carter before, I love watching him fish.

Fishing can require diplomacy. I'm not competitive and try not to fish with people who are. I've fished with serious anglers, guides, professionals, who are in a different class than I am. I don't compare myself with them—their casting and tactics are high-level—I just watch and try to learn something. I can compare their many fish to my few fish, but can't be bothered by that. They say if you're the smartest person in the room, you're in the wrong room. I don't have to be the best angler in the boat. In a perfect world, you appreciate spending time on the water together.

I'm thinking of all this as Joel and I look for birds. Actually, Joel does most of the looking because I'm just enjoying being in the bay. Gulls swirl and plunge. We speed over, slow down, and approach slowly. Joel has a sensor too, and it tells him if fish are present and relatively how deep they are. That only gets us so far. We have to decide if we want to fish shallow or deep, on floating or sinking line. When there are rising fish, coming up and crashing through the bait, they smack the surface of the water. This is more fun—you see the striper take the fly, which is always better. Most fish, however, are farther down, so you've got to make a choice—smaller chance for fish on the surface or better chance for fish on sinking line. This is always a major dividing line between anglers.

If we see any rises, we'll stay on the surface. And that's just what we see. There's a miniature explosion on the water and I cast toward it, then strip in as fast as I can. After a few moments I can see the white of the streamer, then, out of nowhere, a phantom passes it. It looks like a gray ghost against the dark background of the water, like the brushstroke of an action painting, Willem de Kooning in Jamaica Bay. What *was* that? Before I can focus, it streaks back again. A striper. Now it slows just enough to take the fly. I'm in shock as I strip and set the hook.

This is no longer theoretical. The rod bends and the fish heads straight down. I reel in until there's pressure and the fish heads down again, taking out line. "Nice," Joel says. He's caught many more stripers in his life than I have. When he catches a striper, it feels much less random than when I do. "We're in about forty feet of water," he notes. This sounds as if this is supposed to mean something to me. As the fish continues to go down, I realize it's hard to land a fish in deep water, since it can swim farther down where there's more current. After a few minutes it finally comes closer to the boat and we can make out its silver body. When it's next to the boat, Joel grabs the leader. He raises the fish, the whitest stomach, and gunmetal-gray side streaked with black. A big eye. A friendly fish, if I can say that. This is striper fishing. Joel puts the fish back in the water. It wastes no time swimming into the darkness.

I relax and look for more birds. Joel is patient and keeps casting. When we don't see action, he pulls the boat toward other places he knows are good. Joel casts even when fish aren't visibly feeding. This is one reason he catches more fish than I do. He also, like many serious striper anglers, retrieves his line hand over hand, bypassing the reel until a fish is on. When I see this the first time, I'm startled. After he casts, he supports his rod between his arm and his body so both his hands are free. Then he pulls the line with one hand and then the other, just above the reel, as quickly as possible. The fly comes in faster than the way I strip it in, with one hand. I tell myself this extra speed doesn't matter, but plenty of accomplished anglers think it matters to the bass.

We eat lunch in a calm area near some reeds while the boat floats along. In the afternoon, I'm stripping in my conventional way when there's a violent tug on the line. A fish is on and it's pulling harder than the bass. The line starts to come in, and Joel says from the stern, "Bluefish." An interloper! There are more fish than just stripers in Jamaica Bay, many more. One of these is the bluefish. You probably think of the bluefish more on the plate than in the water. It's a strong-tasting, rather oily fish, silver with a dull gray-black. Not very striking, the bluefish looks like a child's drawing of a fish. But it's strong, a voracious eater with very sharp teeth. When bluefish are feeding, it can be a frenzy, and there are stories of them eating anything they see, even if what they see is a beer can.

Robert Hughes, the late, great art critic, did a lot of saltwater fishing off his house on Shelter Island. His advice on cooking bluefish was that it had to happen the day it was caught. He wrote a wonderful short book about his angling life called *A Jerk on One End*. The title refers to the moment when a jerk on one end of the line feels a jerk on the other. It's heartening to think that an art critic could have a house on Shelter Island and his own boat. Those were the days!

Miraculously this bluefish makes it to the boat. It's hooked exactly in the corner of its jaw. If it's not hooked there, it usually breaks off the leader with its alarmingly sharp teeth. You have to put a wire leader on, but Joel thinks the wire leader can spook the bass away. This bluefish is about the size of a miniature dachshund. Where there's one bluefish there's usually another, and quickly Joel has one on the line. He's already put a wire leader on his rig so it won't break. Then he catches a second. Now Joel relaxes too.

The bluefish reminds me of the wildness of Jamaica Bay. It still strikes me as improbable, to be in the middle of all of this so close to the city. It's never predictable: we might catch a striper, might catch a bluefish, might catch anything or nothing. New Yorkers think they're at the center of the world, and then there's a whole other world a short boat ride away.

In the afternoon we head back to the marina. Joel slowly steers the boat into the slip. He drives me to the ferry. When I came this morning, there was only one other person on the deck. Now, in the warm afternoon, there are a dozen. We're all grateful to escape the intensity of the city, if only for a few hours.

I thought I'd return the favor. I book a guide in Montauk. We can fish, and Joel won't have to worry about maneuvering the boat, which is a serious responsibility. Montauk, on the east end of Long Island, has long been an angling outpost—for big boats hauling out to sea targeting bluefin tuna and also, increasingly, for fly anglers.

We are heading out with Brendan, a successful guide who captains a twenty-five-foot center console boat. This boat has plenty of space for everything three people might want to do on the water. Brendan is thin and alert, his beard starting to turn gray, though not as gray as mine. He has a twitchy intensity about him. He's on the water 180 days a year. Everything we've done in Jamaica Bay is now on a larger scale. In Montauk, the marina is bigger, the boats are bigger, the engines are bigger, the water is bigger, the crowds are bigger. What we don't know is if the fish will be bigger. It's 7 a.m. Brendan pulls us slowly into the channel, past Gosman's restaurant, past the pylons. When the water is deep enough, the boat picks up speed.

Now, as laws of angling require, the weather is dicey, as it always is for trips booked in advance. It's a gray day with choppy water. Brendan acts as if this is normal, and out here in the Atlantic it probably is. I don't want to be the one who notes that it requires some serious balance just to make a cast. It might not even occur to Brendan, so naturally does he stand as the boat pitches back and forth.

We head to the point beneath the famous Montauk lighthouse, which was commissioned by George Washington and built in 1796 in a brisk five months. On the easternmost point of the East End, it's kept boats from crashing into the rocks for more than two centuries. The lighthouse is in the process of being repainted, half of the job is finished, pristine white with a wide red stripe across its center. The other half is not painted, the bricks visible through the faded white. There's a vertical line separating the two halves, literally right down the middle. It's uncanny. I stare at it longer, and in the fog and low-lying clouds it feels like the job's been abandoned. The two-toned lighthouse looks like a symbolic landmark, the monumental effort required to keep up appearances on a harsh coast, like some large metaphor from a Werner Herzog film.

I can't look at it too long, however, because it's time to fish. There are already twenty boats along the rip, fishing various areas. Brendan knows the boats and the captains. He has kind words for a few and harsh words for many. He gets on the radio and speaks to some friendly guides. They talk about what's working and possibly, if I'm hearing correctly, exchange a few lurid jokes. Brendan isn't some old-timer. He's living in the modern world, on good terms with chefs, editors, writers. It's certainly good for his professional life to be fluent in these matters, but his skills are enduring ones. He puts you on fish.

As I've mentioned it's not a calm day. I have to keep telling myself that and looking in the distance. There's nothing between us and real water—the horizon is absolute. Maybe it's not the Bahamas, but it's certainly not Wisconsin either. We're fishing in the rip, a force of nature, where two currents converge. The currents push the baitfish here and that brings the bass.

Brendan has a lot to balance. He looks in his binoculars for signs of feeding fish, and he also looks for gulls. He's doing all this while navigating the boat. If he finds them, then he has to work his way through the boats to a good place for us to cast, preferably with the wind at our backs. This is intricate work that he makes look easy. When he does all that, some other boat might come speeding up to the area, and if it arrives too suddenly the sound of the motor will send the fish down. Then Brendan will have more harsh words.

If the fish go down, he has another decision to make. If the boats leave, do we stay and hope the fish return? Or do we go to a new place with few boats (but also fewer gulls and presumably fewer fish)? This intuition, this sense of where the fish will be is what makes a good striped bass angler. It has to do with knowledge established over time — where fish typically feed, the nature of specific currents, how they relate to incoming or outgoing tides.

If viewed from above, the movement of all the boats would look absurd. Like a video game, like Tetris. One moves, another takes its place. Somebody gives up. Somebody still has faith. There's a lot of movement, much of it unnecessary. Brendan is patient. He thinks there are plenty of fish in the area, even if there are gulls only in certain places. I've been casting for about half an hour, a variation of a Clouser minnow that Brendan tied himself.

I'm stripping in when suddenly the line stops. Only a real fish could do that. The line won't move in at all. I try to get the loose line on the reel, because the fish goes on a screaming run, like a bonefish, but stronger. Just as I'm thinking, *This doesn't feel like a bass*, Brendan says "Albie." As I'm processing this, the fish is now two hundred feet away. Another interloper! The false albacore is a smaller relation of the tuna. It looks like a torpedo, a slab of silver, with a dark blue back. The false albacore is all strength, it's hard, like a watermelon, and doesn't wiggle. This one goes straight to the bottom. I love striped bass, but this fight is very different. The fish is definitely dictating the process, *controlling the narrative*, you might say. Which, I have to admit, is my fault. I've only fished for false albacore once before, off Cape Cod. This torpedo is by far the strongest fish I've ever had on the line.

Brendan says later that I have to be more assertive, that I shouldn't let the fish run so much. Once a false albacore thinks it can escape, it gets ideas and will keep going on runs. We're in deep water, and the rip, with its conflicting currents, is making it harder to put pressure on the fish. Finally, it comes up. In the water near the boat, it's dark blue and aquamarine on its back, with a silver stomach. Brendan leans over and grabs the line and hauls the fish up by the tail. Imagine a tuna. Now imagine that tuna shrunk to eight pounds. That's the false albacore, the miniature version of something noble. It's still impressive. It might have a Napoleon complex, I'm not sure. It certainly has delusions of grandeur that might not even be delusions. Fighting one is bracing.

"The albies showed up two days ago and we started catching them yesterday," Brendan says. "That's one reason there are so many boats today." Albies are popular with fly anglers. Albies create a network of informers, and serious anglers cancel plans and head out East as soon as the word is out. We're lucky the timing is right. I relax in the back with a beer. Joel still casts, promptly gets his own albie, and lands it much more quickly than I did mine. It's 9:30 a.m.

The triumphant beer may have been premature considering the choppy water. I presumed it would calm down over the course of the morning, which was based, like many angling premonitions, entirely on desire. So I relax and get my equilibrium, while Joel fishes.

There are a lot of fly fishing guides and their sports are accomplished. It's a commitment to book one of these guides, and casting, in the wind, with big, weighted flies, is not an ideal place to learn. These people take it seriously. It's interesting to stand next to Brendan and hear his take on how other captains handle their boats. There's an ethic here. You have to be sensitive to other anglers, not merely your own desire for action. He disapproves of boats that arrive loudly to an area where people are casting to fish.

From Brendan's point of view, guiding is not just finding fish but navigating the boat. Joel does this well in Jamaica Bay, but this is another level of magnitude. We're jockeying against big boats, with ridiculously large, powerful motors. While steering, Brendan offers gentle reminders: *Don't cast over the boat.* Advice: *May want to change that fly.* He and Joel discuss the Rockaways, where Brendan keeps a boat and has guided for years. *Your name doesn't sound Irish*, Brendan, who's Irish, notes, since that's a common theme among boat owners in Joel's marina.

So Brendan is playing three-dimensional chess. Joel and I each catch a few more albies. In fact, we have a few doubles (when both anglers on a boat have fish on). Brendan stands back trying not to show his satisfaction. In the early afternoon the cluster of boats starts to break up and head their separate ways. The feeding seems to have slowed down and people are making their next plan. Brendan takes us beyond the rip, and we can see grand old houses on the bluff, some with long wooden stairways winding down to the beach below.

We keep casting, though there's less bird activity. It's strange the way you become dependent on these gulls. You start to look for them eagerly, which is funny since seagulls are hardly a beloved animal. Now we look for them desperately. I cast and strip, cast and strip, cast and—a hit. A deep, sustained pull. A good fish but none of the insane runs of earlier. It's a striper. I bring it in. And Brendan calmly grabs the line and pulls in the fish. We don't use nets. I should mention that. When it's close, the guide takes the leader and pulls up the fish. If something truly wild happens, a tuna is involved, the gaff comes out to haul it over the side. My angling career has, in fact, been gaff-free, though not gaffe-free. Now Joel has a fish on. Also a striper. Also good. It's common to catch these fish in close intervals, since they often feed in schools. A deep gray back, vivid black stripes along its silver flank—a vigorous fish.

Fishing in Montauk is different. It doesn't happen in the shadow of New York City, so it doesn't feel so incongruous, so opportunistic. There are no jets, no signs of city life. It feels like being part of a greater tradition that goes back centuries. Though we're intersecting with it in its more rarefied form. Light tackle for pleasure. Not as a livelihood, not for food. The marina is full of many boats whose owners take this seriously, who motor for hours for a chance at a bluefin tuna. They used to sell them on the dock to agents who would freeze them and load them on the next flight to Tokyo. That's no joke. The stakes are different.

It's far from trout fishing. Sometimes you get a glimpse of a wider world, of water as far as you can see. The weather starts to calm down. We continue to move along the shore, where the current is gentler. The sky lightens and feels less imposing. I am sure the sun will come out later that afternoon.

CANADA

ATLANTIC SALMON

Patience

What makes a bad idea *bad*? There's the bad idea that's so crazy that nobody will go along with it, rejected immediately, like expired milk. That bad idea's not dangerous—it safely remains in the realm of unreality, dismissed out of hand. No, the truly bad idea is powerful because it convinces those who know it's bad to go along with it. Because there's a chance, however remote, for deliverance. Long odds make improbable success more attractive, even romantic. A bad idea with potential. Now, that's my kind of bad idea.

Why do I say this? Because Markley suggested a fishing trip that we both knew—and both *agreed*—was a bad idea. After we considered it for a while and came to terms with the fact that it was essentially crazy, that craziness became part of its appeal. Anglers working in tandem get into situations where nobody's editing out ideas that shouldn't be considered in the first place. They reinforce each other and then get into trouble.

The reason we took this trip was simple: the Atlantic salmon. Many shattered dreams lay at the altar of this revered fish. But Markley's father, a member of a small, distinguished angling club on a river in New Brunswick, made us an offer we couldn't refuse: join him at his club for a few days to fish for salmon. I'll keep the location vague—even by the standards of secretive anglers, members of clubs are particularly prone to geographic paranoia. Reveal too many details and never be invited back. As it stands, I probably won't be invited anyway. I didn't exactly bathe myself in glory.

The camp is along a stretch of a storied river, and leases the land from the Crown. Yes, that crown. Every ten years, a club member goes and bids on renewing the lease from a representative of the Queen. At least that's the story. Markley's father had reserved a few days far in advance, as members do each year. We were set to join him in Maine, and then all drive out East together.

A month before, the reports were not promising. The

salmon had not moved up from the ocean into the river to spawn. This fact is not abstract or theoretical. It might be considered, in military parlance, *actionable intelligence*. If the salmon are not there, they're not there, so there's no way to catch them. It's over and done. Do a crossword. Play some cribbage. Sit by the fire. Read a book.

A guide from the club gave Markley regular reports, which he dutifully relayed to me, and we analyzed them for any sign of hope. With a week to go, the fish still hadn't moved into the river. We had time to pull out. There was no disgrace in living to fight the salmon another year, but next year felt so far away. Other groups saw the light and cashed out. A few days before, we *still* could have canceled. Theoretically, we should have been clinical about this, weighed our options and considered the big picture. But acting together, under the vision of salmon, we lost all power of reason. The fact that there didn't seem to be fish in the river didn't slow us down at all. Not one bit.

Oh, and even if the salmon *are* in the river, they remain one of the hardest fish to catch. They are the most mercurial, the most mystical, the most majestic fish. We're talking about the gleaming silver Atlantic salmon here, not its more open-minded and agreeable relative, the Pacific salmon (often striped brilliant red, raised aloft by dining grizzly bears). Go to Alaska and you will have a wonderful time and catch plenty of Pacific salmon. Atlantic salmon are different. They shut you out and break your heart. Lose a good one and it might even break your spirit. They test friendships and bank accounts. They are a noble fish, regal and refined, known as the Fish of a Thousand Casts. And they earned that name when there were a hell of a lot more Atlantic salmon swimming about.

Markley and I had all this information at hand. Nothing was hidden. Still, there was no doubt what we were going to do. We drove up the Maine coastline and into New Brunswick knowing that we should know better. There was still a small chance the salmon would arrive any day. Any day! The difference between a small chance, a remote chance, and no chance is the distinction we're looking at here. In the end, perhaps we didn't look closely enough.

At some deep level we believed, or at least *wanted* to believe, in the possibility. Sometimes that belief is all it takes. The long odds make the story better, after all. But the story, when you're the one telling it, ideally ends with a fish. As we pulled into a nondescript parking lot on a gray October day, at the edge of the middle of nowhere, we had a sense of how it would end. But we still hoped for an outside chance. We still hoped for a plot twist.

The salmon is no ordinary fish. Evelyn Waugh said, "I despise all my children equally." He had seven. You'd expect a parent to say they love all their children equally but some more equally than others. Well, I love all fish equally, but I love the salmon more equally than most. I certainly wanted to catch one more than I did any other fish. And heading up to Canada with Markley, I'd never fished for salmon before. This persistent fact placed me on the modest side of a very important angling experience. I was still green.

The salmon is a storied fish not only because it's beautiful but also because it has what screenwriters might call *a compelling backstory*. Just a reminder about how truly remarkable the salmon is: It grows up in a river, where it spends the first year of its life. Then, as if graduated from college and ready for the wider world, it swims to the ocean, a thousand miles away, where it lives for three or four years. It gets silvery and strong, big and beautiful. What an animal! Then, in one of evolution's great feats, it swims the thousand miles back to the exact river where it was born and heads up it, against the current, where it spawns. Sometimes it returns to the exact same pool, edged by the same riverbank, and finds its childhood home. It does all this without a map.

The salmon's story may be impressive, but it's a striking fish on its own. In a word, silver. Perhaps no living thing is more silver. Breaking water, jumping in the air, water spraying—this is the natural expression of its spirit. Its wide back is a strip of black, then its side reveals small black spots spaced close together or far apart.

Salmon migrations make land along the rivers they pass through incredibly valuable. Sometimes these rivers' banks are owned by a club or a lodge where the most promising weeks are in high demand. Anglers speak of salmon rivers like the Miramichi in Canada or the Alta in Norway with the reverence usually reserved for first-growth Bordeaux. And, as with first-growth Bordeaux, you're going to pay a painful amount for the pleasure.

Money complicates fly fishing. With a rod, a reel, a sense of ingenuity, and some difficulty, the sport can be a relative bargain. More often, it's expensive. Sometimes luridly so. Money buys access to places where the fishing is known to be good. People can make up their own minds about what makes sense for them. I have friends who collect valuable bamboo rods they don't even use. Markley meanwhile became obsessed with a $50 rod made in China. "It's not *that* bad," he says. "And for fifty dollars, you can't beat it."

You can set down your platinum card and book a place on a helicopter to a remote lake, or you can hike for hours for free in a national park. To me, the danger of high prices for lodges, guides, camps, and the rest is that it distorts the experience. By all means, pay what you want to be where you want to be, but that can cloud expectations about the fishing. There's no short line from a credit card to catching a fish. It might put you in a better position to succeed, but looking at the situation like an equation ignores the complications and the uncertainty inherent in angling. All of which is to say that you have to come to terms with the difficulty of catching a salmon, and come to terms, in the less romantic sense, with the cost. That can be hard to do.

This inconvenience can all be avoided if you're a member of the British Royal Family and a salmon river flows through your ancestral estate. This may be why royals have long enjoyed salmon fishing in Scotland. The rest of us have to move to find the fish. Salmon travel a long way, and they inspire anglers to travel just as far. Anglers have been going after salmon for decades. Some of their names echo through the sport: Charles Ritz (son of César, the hotelier), spent his time going around Europe, catching immense salmon the size of dining room tables. Lee Wulff helped popularize salmon fishing in America in the 1950s when he was on television and publishing seminal books on the subject, still referred to today. Ted Williams, his baseball career behind him, spent most of his time fishing. He loved catching salmon.

People obsessed with salmon fishing, in my experience, have the clearest sense of the vagaries of the sport. Salmon stories involve sighing and wistful laughter, like an old relative in a Chekhov play. This is because salmon remain the most mysterious fish. We follow their movements and study them intensely. But, and I can't put too fine a point on this: *Nobody knows why they take a fly.* When they swim up a river to spawn, they do not eat. And yet, on rare, blessed occasions, they will take a fly.

This is a natural phenomenon that invites speculation and conspiracy theories, like Stonehenge or crop circles. The fact that it's unexplained doesn't inhibit anglers from coming up with wild ideas. On the contrary, it provokes them. Anglers abhor a factual vacuum. The vacuum is created because we want to know why a salmon takes a fly that swings in front of it. It's a question that's launched a thousand books.

Salmon take a fly because they're territorial. Or salmon take a fly because they're annoyed. Or they do it because they simply want to spawn. A salmon takes a fly when it arrives in a certain angle at a certain speed. There's endless talk about why they take a fly. But that doesn't matter, because most of the time they aren't taking a fly at all. That leaves you standing with your rod, trying to come up with some theory about their extreme, almost heroic, indifference to what you're doing.

Why do people go through all of this? Because, once

hooked, a salmon will run, a salmon will jump, and that may be the most beautiful sight in the entire sport. That vision is so strong that it hijacked my sense of reason and took me to Canada.

Compared to catching a salmon, driving into New Brunswick is a mundane affair. We're putting in miles on a highway on a gray day. After a few hours, we descend into the Miramichi River Valley, and things get more serious. We see hints of angling life. There are signs for access to the legendary Miramichi, one of the storied salmon rivers. We park outside Doak's, a renowned fishing store, which is, naturally enough, in Doaktown.

There are many types of fly fishing stores, the same way there are many types of bookstores (or used to be). There's the small, highly personal store, unapologetically eccentric, that implies what they don't have isn't worth having. Then there's the authoritative store, and anything you might want they will definitely have. "W.W. Doak and Sons Ltd. Fly Fishing Tackle" is the latter. An institution in a gray wooden building on Main Street, it's been run by the Doaks since opening in 1946. They carry an exhaustive collection of flies, fly-tying material, fly boxes, not to mention rods, reels, boots, hats. It has the easy assurance of a recognized authority. The people working there meticulously tie salmon flies, and are perfectly nice. Like a record store clerk, the fly shop employee has been known to raise an eyebrow at the outsider or perceived non-expert. Not so at Doak's.

The counter is covered with row after row of famous salmon flies with names like professional wrestlers: Black Bear, Preacher, Green Widow, Undertaker, Shady Lady. A salmon fly is usually on a long hook, wrapped with black thread, with some dash of sparkle and color. These flies are quite pretty, and naturally anglers are incredibly partial to a certain one for reasons of past success or straight-up superstition. Markley assures me I can borrow some of his flies. But I lurch around the store like a child on a sugar high, buying flies based purely on impulse. I feel a strong connection with something called a Green Bomber. I stare at the Green Bomber—it looks like two hairy pencil erasers stuck together—and wonder if it will change my life. It just might.

We leave Doak's and head farther east into New Brunswick. Markley and his father have a detailed discussion about where we'll meet the guides. I think of early trips in Wisconsin with Dave when we would show up in the middle of nowhere and Lorne would already be waiting to meet us. Dave always had unexpected secrets—sometimes we would stop in a remote part of the woods and he would lead us to an old boat he kept hidden and chained to a tree. This feels like that—there's the knowledge that Markley and his father share after years of these trips. I'm the outsider with everything still to learn.

Apparently this rendezvous with the guides used to be in the parking lot of a diner. Markley says the diner had very good poutine, which sounds a little bit like a threat since he knows I intend to spend my time in Canada poutine-free. Poutine, like scrapple (which Markley also likes, oddly, since he's a devotee of vegetarian Indian cuisine), is something I try to avoid in my life. Markley mentions in passing that the chef at the fishing camp makes very good poutine, which is also alarming, since then, presumably, I'll be forced to eat it just to be polite. After some consideration, we pull into the nondescript parking lot of a veterans' hall, empty except for two men standing in front of a truck. It's like a criminal meeting.

The two men are our guides, Denys and John. They have an air of unassuming competence. They remind me of the men who live near our cabin in Wisconsin, woodworkers who build houses and smoke chickens in fireplaces they make. The guides speak the flat English of French Canadians. I always think this makes them sound polite, but maybe it's just because Canadians are polite. Markley's father and the guides greet each other warmly. He's been a member of the club since the 1970s, and has fished here nearly every year since then. It's a time for reunions and bonhomie. I just want to see the river. I'm ready for my education to begin.

We load everything from our car into the back of their truck. Duffel bags with sweaters, flannel shirts, long underwear, rain gear. Rods, waders, boots, fly boxes, bottles of scotch and wine that we *forgot* to declare when we crossed the border, books we won't read—everything we might need for three days of fishing. I wonder why we don't just take Markley's jeep. "Most cars don't like the road we're taking," Denys says cryptically.

Denys is the head guide. He has a graying mustache and the aura of being in command. He's sharp and hard to read. You wouldn't want to play poker with him. We climb into his truck and drive toward the camp. We're on a dirt road that turns into a field of blueberry bushes, then we come to the top of a steep, steep hill, like the apex of a roller coaster. The road ceases to be a road in the traditional sense—really, just a slope of boulders. "Slope" makes it sound gentle—this is more menacing: dark gray rocks etched with two faint parallel tread marks that gently weave through them, like a slalom course. The tires on Denys's truck, we learn, are six times the thickness of regular tires, reinforced specifically for this drive. He drives confidently down the hill, though, as slowly as the truck can go, one rotation at a time. The passengers in the back bounce with every turn. You could get out and walk faster.

We arrive at the camp, which is direct in its assessment of our needs. Just two wooden buildings painted pale gray. One is for us, the sports, the other, across a dirt path, is for the guides. They're similar except theirs has a kitchen, and a lingering cloud of cigarette smoke. Both buildings have kerosene lamps. Neither has power. Of course that means no internet and no cell service. We've gone a very long way to get to a place that doesn't have electricity, to try to land a famously elusive fish. People have gone years and spent thousands of dollars to travel to *not* catch salmon. Will I be one of those poor unfortunates?

I drop my bags in the bedroom and walk over to survey the river. It's narrow—thirty feet across, the length of a relaxed cast—there's barely a current. It has a studied modesty and even feels gentle. Along the banks are the newly yellow October leaves. Across from us are spare birch trees; their white bark stands out like long chalk marks in front of the dark pines. The more I stare at it, the more I begin to lose focus, hypnotized by the water's unhurried movement. Rivers are reassuring that way. What could possibly go wrong here? Whose morale could possibly be taken, bent, twisted, and crushed?

We settle in at the camp. It's a time of good intentions. Morale is high, perhaps higher than is justified under the circumstances. I sense the past in the simple wooden buildings set above the river, that the people who come here really care about this place. The main room is dominated by a stone fireplace, the only source of heat. There's an immense logbook, which serves as an unofficial history of the club. Every salmon that's been caught here has been entered in that book, in the meticulous handwriting of previous generations. Markley's father's name is written on many pages, and so are the fish he's caught. There are photo albums of members holding prized salmon. There are no photos of people holding nothing, no photos of people on the brink of tears.

The wooden walls are bare except for a few illustrated posters of *The Fish of Canada*, their color fading. There are framed photos, no doubt put up by the members who took them. These are looked upon by other members with mild annoyance. Either because they're taken by an amateur nature photographer with an outsize assessment of his own ability or are of a member grinning a little too broadly, holding a twenty-pound salmon. They generate the décor friction that's another honored fishing club tradition.

CANADA

The camp is its own little world, run by the guides and Pierre, the chef. Pierre works the kitchen intensely and then brings meals over to a large table in our cabin. He and the guides help one another with all the responsibilities of maintaining a camp in this isolated setting. There are occasional visits to the small town up the steep hill. It's a communal experience—they all smoke and, judging from the rosy cheeks they have in the evening and sounds emanating from their cabin, are not abstaining from Canadian whiskey.

On our first night we have a fire in the cabin. With the sun down it's properly cold, the way you would imagine it to be in Canada. I pray the heat extends to the modest bedrooms. Suddenly, Pierre bursts into the room rather wildly, carrying a tray with two dozen Beausoleil oysters from the nearby coast. They gleam under the kerosene lamps. It feels like we're detached from the world, a hundred years in the past. I try one. It's about the best oyster I've ever eaten.

The next morning we go outside and start rigging up our rods. This is still one of my favorite times of any trip. Nothing has been marred. It's like opening day in a baseball season—no losses yet, no unearned runs. John strolls over and glances at one of our fancy rods and somebody's new reel. He raises an eyebrow as if he's impressed. He really means: You think this will help? He sees it with every group. The latest technology meant to bring order to the inherently chaotic angling universe. But we need that irrationality, and guides know it.

Fishing here is a simple equation. You go to a pool, each

one is named, and fish it. If the salmon are in the river, they'll be in the pools, not between them. You don't wander. You don't improvise. Salmon fishing involves a ritual—you cast across the river and let the fly swing until it's pointing directly downstream, parallel to the bank. Then you take two steps down and do it again. You cover water so every fish in the pool will see that fly. It is systematic, rigorous, without romance. Cast, swing, and step down. Nothing? Step down three feet, same cast, same swing. Probably same result.

You don't change flies or keep casting to a specific spot. You're not encouraged to get too invested in a certain lie. Don't become attached to anything. You don't even want to think too hard. Your job is to cover water. Once you've established your settings—fly, angle, distance—then, in many ways, you're a casting machine set on repeat. How long would you be willing to do this? How much monotony can you handle just for the remote chance of catching a fish? If you have to ask that, perhaps salmon fishing is not for you. And that's all right, salmon fishing is not for everybody. Even the people who love it know it's insane.

How many casts does it take to catch a salmon? Somewhere between *I stopped counting* and *infinity*. I try to stay alert in the face of a healthy amount of tedium. Then I ask myself if there's such a thing as a healthy amount of tedium. These are the thoughts you must banish from your head. At first, there's something meditative about this way of fishing. I get over that quickly. I don't want to lose focus. I have to be ready if a salmon finally takes my beloved Green Bomber.

That's when the excitement comes. The guides leap into

action and streak down the river if the salmon runs, then help you land it. That's the exception. Most often they just stand a healthy distance from you while you cast, sometimes taking a break from a cigarette to offer cryptic advice. *That's a good speed*, you might hear from behind you. And you sense that your drift is indeed on an effective line where the current took it at an agreeable speed. But it ends as all the others before it, and then the guide returns to watching you not catch fish. They're analysts who specialize in men on the brink of frustration, even cracking up. If one of these men finally catches a salmon then loses it, that frustration breaks into acute despair. Glory turns to tragedy in an instant, a mood swing so wild you'll remember it the rest of your life.

I'm ready to go with my Green Bomber. I ask John if the Bomber looks good, to see if he shares my enthusiasm, figuring he'll have some local intelligence. He says, perfectly kindly, that yes, the Green Bomber is good. "We might try something orange later." The delivery is so neutral it implies my love for the Bomber is misplaced, but also that changing a fly is just as useless. This is no doubt true. But if I'm going to cast the Green Bomber a hundred times, please allow me the illusion that it's a good idea. I'd like to pretend I have some small control over this process. These guides are not here to make you feel better about yourself. They're like bookies familiar with human frailty and slightly unimpressed with what that frailty makes men do. I don't want to say they're disapproving, but you half expect them to take a drag on a cigarette and say, What's the point, we're all going to die anyway.

I'm trying to sort out what I need to know on the off chance I catch a salmon. Markley says a large salmon will often stay on the bottom of the river for so long you swear it's a log or a rock. Then, after thirty seconds, when you finally give up and decide it's a log, it will bolt downstream, and promptly break off your line, leaving you traumatized until the shock wears off, when it will be replaced by a slow-burning fury that can last a year or two. I can't believe all this could come out of the mild river in front of us. The water's dark, slightly stained, rocks come into focus as you stare at it. It's the presence of salmon that will change its character.

In a perfect world, as the fly swings down, you feel a knock. The big point of discussion, for the first-time salmon angler, is the take, *the knock*. In some rivers a salmon takes the fly from the surface in plain sight. In our situation, the fly is below the surface and any take will be invisible. You won't see it, just feel it. "Like hitting a stone," I'm told. There are stones in the river, couldn't a fly catch one of those stones? It could. "But if the stone was alive." Now, this is the sort of mystical advice that's both profound and useless. Somebody else makes it simpler: "You'll know." But would I?

This discussion is at once vital and alarmingly vague, a specialty among anglers. After all this casting, all the swinging, all the waiting, you finally feel the knock, and what do you do? The first thing you would *not* do is raise your rod, as most any angler would do. No, you would feel the knock, and you, showing an astonishing amount of self-control, would let the salmon return with the fly to its holding place. After the first shocking impact, this doing nothing would require a heroic amount of patience. The salmon would turn down, then start to pull, and the line would head out from the reel. Finally, you could act. Now, gripping the reel, you would stop the line and set the hook. In a theoretical world, the fun would then begin. Did you follow all that? I'm trying to, but it isn't easy.

So I step out on the bank of the river. This is the opposite of being in the Bahamas, where Markley and I fished before. There, it was hot, and we could see endless flats in every direction. Now it's chilly, we're in a valley surrounded by forests. There you cast rarely, only when you see a bonefish. Now we cast again and again to, we hope, invisible salmon that will make themselves visible. There's a chill in the air. The grass of the banks is starting to turn brown. It feels like the end of the accommodating season, real weather will arrive soon, nature will exert its control.

This gray area about the knock is explored fairly early on and in somewhat controversial circumstances. Because I catch a rock. It's dead solid—it might as well be a grand piano. It does not move, it does not budge, it does not do anything a salmon might do. I wait and wait, it does not move an inch. Do they use the metric system in Canada? It does not move 2.54 centimeters. I just want to make that very clear. Do I sound defensive? Why would I sound defensive? I'm not defensive. I'm offended you would even think I was defensive. You mean, I sound defensive because I had a salmon and lost it? That's crazy. It was a rock. It was clearly a rock.

Well, not according to Denys. Denys, who was nowhere near the situation as it unfolded, tells John later, in clear earshot of myself, "Looks like we had one this morning."

My ears burn at his Canadian understatement. This disagreement about whether or not there was a knock felt like a horror movie when one character swears the house is haunted and nobody believes him. I can hear the voiceover of the trailer in my mind:

Coming Soon
In a world where things are not what they seem
Where water hides secrets and holds the power
One man knew what he felt
And fought for the truth no matter the cost.
A new vision of horror in the Canadian wilderness
Brace yourself for . . .
The Knock
Rated R for Trauma

Now that I'm indoctrinated in what may or may not have been a knock, I try to allow my frustration to turn into something more positive. Later that morning, on the downswing, I feel a much livelier knock and hello, what's this? It's a fish. I know this is a fish, it moves right away. I pull in loose line and set the hook. It comes in a little easier than I expect for the storied salmon. Where's the run? Where's the majestic jump? As I reel in a silver fish jumps, smaller than I imagined. "A grilse," Denys says in a tone that cannot be considered congratulatory. He has moved down beside me with the net. This confirmation takes some of the vim out of the proceedings. A grilse is a one-year-old salmon that usually hasn't gone out to sea yet. It's small and pretty but not really what we're here for. I fight it fairly aggressively.

This grilse jumps again, right in front of us, and throws the hook. It quickly swims back into the pool.

That's good enough for me. We saw the fish, I fought it, brought it ten feet from us. It wasn't the fish we wanted anyway. Denys says something I can't make out. "What's that?" I ask. "Might want to let it run," he intones calmly. Jeeves asking Wooster "Are you intending to wear that dinner jacket in public?" could not be more devastating. I think maybe he misunderstands the situation. The grilse hadn't gone on a run and broken off. It could jump and throw the hook anywhere, near or far. "He's right," Markley offers, seemingly out of nowhere, really piling on. "You don't want to be too aggressive with any salmon." Good grief. I didn't think I was being aggressive at all. I don't want to press the point and don't feel that I'm in a position to. Apparently, salmon education doesn't come slowly, but all at once, whether you want to it to or not.

The next day we drive to another beat. The truck climbs the rocky hill as slowly as it descended. We drive through a field, past more blueberries and stumps of trees which were logged the year before. For a few minutes we have phone service, and, naturally enough, a day's worth of banal information piles up in inboxes. I think, *What could I possibly have missed?* I have no urgent business, I'm trying to be out of reception, in the moment and all that.

I read, to my pleasure, an email from an editor saying a book of mine is going to be reprinted, then, to my horror, that I should send any corrections by *the end of the day.* Yes, there were a few typos (to my abiding shame—where was the copy editor is what I want to know!). I have to respond before we lose reception. I don't want to ask Denys to stop. I came to Canada to get away from everything, now the world won't let me escape. Or maybe I care about certain things in New York more than I care to admit—what are a few misspellings, after all? I try to send an email before we descend to the river, I don't even know if it goes through. I just want to forget New York and focus on salmon, on the next knock.

After the boulder hill a dirt road seems like the Autobahn. We reenter the forest and drive partway down a gentler hill, then walk the rest of the way to a long pool that curves in a bend around a grassy peninsula. This is where we'll start and then fish down. In what seems like a good spot—though they all seem equally good to my novice eye—I quickly feel a take. Not the big one, I can tell right away. Fairly quickly, no doubt more quickly than Denys would prefer, I bring in another grilse. It's good to have action, even if we aren't catching the main attraction. The grilse is pretty, to be sure. It's silver and black, like the older version of itself, though perhaps a little less . . . shimmery, from life at sea.

Denys nets the grilse and states authoritatively that it's two and three-quarter pounds. He's very careful not to allow me the comfort of rounding up to a three-pound grilse. It takes considerably more effort to say *two and three-quarter pounds* than it does to say *three pounds.* Yet Denys could not be clearer. My grilse is a quarter pound short. This is particularly curious because guides, understanding the delicate psyches of their sports, are some of the great rounders up. A fourteen-inch trout becomes a *fifteen-, even a sixteen-incher* by the end of the day. Not this time. Not this guide. Not this grilse.

I consider this situation in more detail that evening when I pick up the logbook, as every angler here does at the end of the fishing day. This tradition dates back through the club's history. I hold this large volume, the leather cover faded, the pages yellowed, and feel connected, in a small way, to all the people who came before me. It's like when you sign in to the register on your first visit to a Savile Row tailor. Though thankfully the tailors keep your measurements separately. Here, all dimensions are down in plain view in black and white.

I can't help but look at the size of other salmon caught here. They're written in ink, next to the date, the name of the pool, and the weight of the fish. There's a space for other details about time of day, the fly, anything that might add to your glory or at the least help anglers who want to know what fly has been working recently and which pools have been productive. Members, upon arriving, generally look at this book very closely, even more closely than at the décor. I can easily imagine them paging through and getting slightly envious at the successes others had. Not that I'm susceptible to such vanity. Not at all.

I note that no grilse on my page is under three pounds. Interesting. There are none on the previous page either. Even more interesting. Suddenly, possessed with the fervor of Indiana Jones poring over the grail diary, I start to flip through the entire book. I turn through the 2010s, and round out the millennium back to 2000. I look through the

1990s, my college years, and back to the 1970s, when I was born. It's a massive volume, with many pages and many more salmon. I'm possessed. I run my finger down the column where the weight of each fish is dutifully listed. I turn every last page.

My two-and-three-quarter-pound grilse is the smallest recorded fish in the history of the club. I almost feel like I should write the Queen herself and inform her of this distinction on her family's water. I deserve some commemoration, if not a knighthood, at least something framed with a royal seal. "The Sweetest Grilse" sounds like a poem children might recite in Shropshire.

The Sweetest Grilse
Reel'd in a-flounder
How wee he is
Two-and-three-quarter-pounder

I have to enter my name in the book, and leave an honest account of my day. I'm certain Denys will make sure that I don't enter three pounds next to my grilse, like a fact checker at the *New Yorker*. In the comment section next to the entries, which other anglers have used as a chance to elaborate on their triumphs, I am at a loss. Beneath "a tremendous fish" or "silver beauty" I write "room for improvement" and close the book.

At breakfast, in the clear light of day, I reflect on my distinction. I'm not sure how I feel about catching the smallest grilse in the history of the club. But for some reason I'm glad I didn't catch the second smallest grilse.

• • •

It's our last morning. The air is heavy, the sky low and gray. We know a storm is arriving—rain, turning to snow, around noon. This takes on some urgency as we'll have to ascend the boulder hill, and with too much precipitation the truck will struggle with the climb. Other than the fact that we might be stuck in the camp, and nobody's caught a salmon, not even had a knock, there's no pressure. Really, none at all.

Markley embraces this. As a certain type of enlightened angler he doesn't mind not catching a salmon. In fact, he seems to relish it. Though, under questioning, he admits catching a twenty-five-pounder a few years earlier, though he seems almost embarrassed about this past triumph, as if it was somehow in questionable taste. It's better to catch a fish and say it doesn't matter than to not catch a fish and say it doesn't matter. That salmon gives him perspective and warm memories. I have neither. If I'd landed a salmon the size of a park bench, then I wouldn't mind getting shut out either.

We return to a long pool we fished the first day. Now I'm starting to develop my own theories. I'm more aware of the different angles to drift the fly and the speed that feels right to me. Naturally, this can't be confirmed, but I have a better sense of what's at stake and how experienced salmon anglers would approach matters. I also have unfounded theories about where a fish might be holding. Light rain begins to fall. No knocks.

The rain is now snow. It falls steadily and melts as it

lands. I keep moving down the pool, casting and swing-ing. I begin to embrace this ritual. I realize it's part of the process, even if that process leads to yet another swing. The waiting gives salmon fishing its meaning, the casts and drifts run together. That's the theory anyway, and it starts to make more sense. Another swing, then another. Still nothing. After an hour the snow stops melting: it rests on the pines in a wall of white.

The snow feels like a curtain coming down on our trip—we have half an hour to drive back to camp, load the truck, and climb the boulders—but it's lovely just being in the val-ley and knowing our time here is ending. This is when anglers are beholden to romantic visions. If there was ever a moment to catch my first salmon, now is the time. I know better. Markley breaks down his rod. He's done. The guide heads back to start the truck, showing a definitive lack of belief or at least a clear-eyed view of the situation. He leaves the net with us in case of a miracle. Or maybe just to taunt me.

One last cast. My fly drifts through the pool. Snow is everywhere, curtains of it, like an endless roll of Japanese paper. The river is still calm. I look at Markley. It really is time to go. He smiles, then nods. There's still time. I cast across the river and the line swings down invisible through the falling snow.

MAINE

BROOK TROUT

Persistence

My favorite highway sign is in the northeast corner of America. It's large—spanning all three lanes of I-95—and is the familiar green. It says simply: "All Maine Points." This is concise yet open-ended, full of possibility, because Maine is full of possibility. There's so much in Maine— rocky coasts and clear lakes, black bears and brook trout,

Winslow Homer's studio and E. B. White's farm. None of this is mentioned on the sign. It doesn't have to be. Our imagination does the rest.

We have a strong image of Maine in our minds. It starts when we're young. Our parents read us *Blueberries for Sal* (I still remember the sound the berries make going into Sal's pail: *kuplink, kuplank, kuplunk*). As slightly older children, we read *Charlotte's Web* on our own. Like many people, I love those books. My Maine connection continued because I went to college here, in ancient times. I didn't, alas, spend that time fishing. In retrospect, I wish I'd minored in angling. But I had more local interests at the time.

One of those interests was the Blue Goose, a small bar, on Sabattus Street at the edge of campus, where seniors would go, drink beer, and play foosball. Then the locals would come and slap their quarters down on the table slightly louder than necessary. They had winners. Sometimes they'd spray WD-40 onto the handles to increase their speed, which seemed like a serious escalation. Then they would throttle the college boys, which they enjoyed a great deal. Who could blame them?

The Blue Goose shared a door with Luigi's Pizzeria. They delivered to the bar, and it wasn't unknown for a pizza to arrive at our back booth after midnight. Luigi's had a policy I've never seen before or since: All their pizzas were served with meat. It looked like ham. I think it was ham. For all I know, it was ham. It still came as a surprise. "There must be some confusion," I said, and was directed to small letters at the bottom of the menu which read, in what may be a first in the English language: ALL PIZZAS

SERVED WITH MEAT. It lacks some of the rhetorical judgment of NO SALAD AS A MEAL, which is inscribed in English
at the top of Brasserie Lipp's menu in Paris. (The fact that
it's not written in French tells you a lot about the two countries and their approach to food.)

Once indoctrinated at Luigi's, you ordered a cheese
pizza with no meat. Which cost extra, a policy I'm still
coming to terms with. I don't want to say that the Blue
Goose is symbolic of Maine. But it is *in* Maine, and symbolic of something. Perhaps it's just that Maine has its own
way of doing things. It can be fancy or gritty, often in close
proximity. That dynamic gives Maine its muscular charm.

For a small state, Maine is pretty big. I'm going to cover a
lot of ground on my drive up to Libby Camps, in the Maine
North Woods. It's farther north than you've been in Maine,
unless you're from Caribou, on the Canadian border. It's
farther north than anywhere in Vermont or New Hamp-
shire. Hell, it's farther north than Montreal. It's up there,
and that's part of the romance.

It's good to be on the road here and I take my time. I
leave Portland in the morning and drive north on Route 1.
This is a less direct route than the interstate and that's good,
the scenery makes up for the lost time. Route 1 is full of
activity—antiques barns, ice cream stands, marine outfitters, stores that specialize in sweaters or quilts or medical
marijuana. I drive up the hill to Wiscasset, with its beautiful
wooden houses painted pretty New England colors. Then
I descend into the charming town along the water. On the

right is Sprague's, which opens at 11 a.m., the perfect time for an early lobster roll, crab roll, or whatever it seems too early for. This is what the English call elevenses, though I doubt they were referring to shellfish.

Leaving Wiscasset, I cross the bridge over the Sheepscot River, and it feels like the Maine of my imagination. Farther up Route 1, in Waldoboro, is Moody's Diner, an institution since it opened in 1927. I now consider my 11 a.m. visit to Sprague's to have been a late breakfast. It's been half an hour, so this, I decide, will be an early lunch. I find a seat at the counter. Did I have a clam roll thirty minutes after I had a lobster roll? I'd rather not say. If I did, then it would have been for research purposes only.

Moody's is the rare diner where you can eat seafood with confidence—they sell local lobster, crab, and the rest of it. They make everything here—it's the type of place that's rightfully proud of its pie. I have to admit the blueberry pie looks good. Pie does seem like a lot, though. Pie's really gilding the lily. No, pie's too much. But the pie case is right in front of my seat, right in my line of sight. No, I draw the line at midday pie. I ask for my bill.

I get a piece to go.

A fishing trip begins before the fishing begins. I love the fishing itself, of course, but I love the anticipation and being in a place with a strong sense of itself. Fishing in Maine means brook trout. I know this list is getting long, but the brook trout may really be the most beautiful fish. It might be what you think of as a trout even if you don't know brook trout. In the simplest terms it's green and red. But what a green and what a red! The green is deep, the color of the forest, along its back and sides. The stomach is vibrant red. Not red exactly, more where red and orange meet. Small yellow spots send it all into relief.

Brook trout like clear, cold water, their presence indicates the health of a lake or river. It's reassuring to catch one in a beloved stream, it means the water is clean. They aren't mercurial, like brown trout, which are calculating and ornery. The brook trout takes a more direct approach, if it wants something it will eat it. It's not reluctant and coy. It's not a mysterious fish, it's just itself, and that's more than enough.

Brook trout are found in the Northeast, and I associate them with Maine. When they're small, they're at their most vivid, a six- or eight-inch brook trout looks like it's made of lacquer, like a Japanese miniature. They can get to be large enough that they're described in pounds. Most trout are long, thin, and measured by length. This is because a twenty-inch brown trout sounds more impressive than a one-and-a-half-pound trout. It's more descriptive too, a trout's length does describe more than its weight. When weight makes a better impression, anglers revert to pounds, migrating, as always, to the most flattering terms possible. A four-pound brook trout is indeed impressive. If I'd ever caught one that size, I would certainly tell people about it. Making very clear it weighed four pounds—for clarity's sake, naturally.

When a brook trout gets that large, it gets a bit of a belly and looks round and decadent, like a successful mob boss.

I prefer them thinner and more streamlined. That may be because I've never caught a huge brook trout. Brook trout are also native fish in New York, close to where I live. It's one of our fish, it wasn't introduced here from someplace else, like brown trout (which came from Germany). It feels good to catch a fish in its native area. It expresses something about the place you're in. That's one reason that brook trout are so beloved. Catching one in Maine feels as natural as can be.

My car is full of essentials. Rods, of course, and reels, waders, boots, flies, and anything you might need for brisk frost in the mornings and determined sun in the afternoon. I take the exit to Ashland and drive due west along a narrow road that rises to a bluff. To the south is Mount Katahdin, the highest point in the state, which Thoreau tried and failed to climb. To the north are dramatic rolling fields. It's impressive. Farm stands sell potatoes. The area produces a lot of potatoes. Children used to be excused from school for two weeks to help in the fields, according to one of the guides, who used to pick them himself, as a boy, for a quarter a barrel.

I arrive in Ashland behind a school bus, which stops at a solitary house. Two boys get out and the bus makes a U-turn, not something you see often. Most school bus routes are planned to limit the moving violations. Then I realize the paved road turns to dirt. This is the end of the line. The dirt conveys a barrier—cross this threshold and enter a more direct, more self-sufficient time. Are you using satellite maps? Listening to a podcast? You're about to leave reception. The dirt road begins.

I consider it a historical signpost when a dirt road is paved. It's a sign of progress, or a sign of something. Old-timers at our cabin in Wisconsin say, "I remember when Plummer Road was dirt!" It's paved now, and sadly renamed to 180th or 375th Avenue. We still call it Plummer Road. I remember talking to Carter about this, he knew the road when it was dirt—and cars had no power steering. There's one extreme hairpin turn that still surprises me and requires close attention. An old car would require even more attention. "Once, my great-grandmother drove off the road at that turn," I told him. "May Stuart used to drive off it annually," he replied in his monotone.

I arrive at a gate to the North Woods. A man emerges from a small building. My car has created a faint cloud of dust. This flinty old-timer helps sign me in and collects the entry fee. He's keen to discuss the area and would be happy if you stay awhile. He's very appealing, but I have to go. I'm feeling the pull of the camp.

The Maine North Woods is a 3.5-million-acre wilderness that extends all the way to Canada. I'm embarrassed to say that I thought it was a state park—the name was so impressive. In fact, the Maine North Woods are privately held, owned primarily by a group of timber interests. They built the dirt roads for their immense logging trucks. It's an interesting balance. It's open to the public, but its operating principle is logging. When I'm in a beautiful forest, I look at it as a natural resource not a financial one. This is a more intense moral consideration than I'm expecting on a relaxing trip to the woods.

I've settled into the dirt road groove, so to speak, when a tall creature runs in front me. I just see haunches. It's darker than a deer and thinner than a bear. I come closer and make out a young moose. It doesn't have antlers yet, the moose's body is small for such long legs—it's lanky, like an awkward teenager. This is June, when the blackflies are dense in the woods, and the moose wants to escape to the road. I learn later that year-old moose leave their mothers at this time each year, so there are a lot of them around. I slow down. The moose doesn't deviate from its path, trotting along with no intention of moving off of the road. I realize I'll have to pass it, the road isn't that wide, and as I pick up speed it finally yields. I look in the rearview mirror and the moose is back in the road again. I pull away and say goodbye to the welcome committee.

There's more dirt, a lot more. It just keeps going. How far? About twenty miles. How long is that? About an hour in your own car. Less in a rental. It's worth it. After the dirt road, Libby Camps feels like a proper civilization, its own miniature city. It's a series of log buildings set on a point that projects into Lake Millinockett. The main lodge is welcoming. It has a wide porch, a large dining room, a kitchen, and a fly shop. This is the only place that has power—it runs on a generator from 5 a.m. until around 9 p.m. There's no cell service. Now guests clamor for a stronger Wi-Fi signal, which is spotty but can be found in certain areas. This circle of reception is where you find the people up from Boston and New York.

There's a cabin, where the guides sleep. The porch is covered with waders, jackets, and boots hanging to dry. This is a place that a child would dream of, even though it's inhabited by middle-aged men. The cabin feels like it lacks adult supervision, which is attractive to anglers away from home. The camp is suspended in a state of young imaginations, which still exerts its pull.

Behind the guide cabin is the icehouse. One day every January the staff heads out onto the lake and they cut large blocks of ice with a chainsaw. They dip the blade in olive oil so it doesn't get stuck. Then they stack the immense blocks, each about the size of a shoe box, using giant tongs that a previous Libby made a hundred years ago. They fill the icehouse then cover the top layer with cedar chips, to slow the melting process, losing just one row over the course of each year.

When you arrive at your cabin—there are about ten around the property—there's a YETI cooler on the deck holding one of these immense blocks. It's a very satisfying sight. The ice is clear and has surprising depth. I know you've seen ice before, but I never do at this scale and this clarity—it seems ancient. Inside the cabin is a large stove and some wood. When lit, the place really heats up. There are kerosene lamps, just turn on the gas, light a match, and then you're ready to party like it's 1899.

There are stacks of wood everywhere, a gas pump, power tools and supplies laying around. If something is broken, they fix it. It makes experts of the staff. Nobody else is coming to repair the roof. That leads to straightforward construction and simple solutions. This architecture and design endure because they work. If you're a fan of log cabins and stone fireplaces, as I am, you'll like this place too.

The camp has been in the Libby family for four generations, it's a family where you learn to fly float planes when you get to be a certain age. These endearing machines are hitched to their dock with a rope, as nonchalantly as sailboats. The camp has three float planes, tied up to three docks, and they sit in a row like ducklings. One is from the 1950s, with just two seats, made of canvas and painted bright yellow. I touch its wing, it feels like an old canoe, pliant but sturdy. Not so sturdy that I want to fly in it.

I wake up to find the lake covered in dense white fog. After breakfast, it still hasn't burned away. There's not enough visibility for the plane to take off. Nobody seems too bothered, and I ask Todd, the guide, when we might expect to leave, so I can be nearby. "When you can see the mountain on the far side of the lake," he says. This is a less scientific answer than I hoped for. When flying is involved, I prefer somebody refers to something with a screen and a keyboard. At least get on a radio, squint meaningfully, and say "Roger that."

After half an hour, the sky clears. Time to go. I've never been in a float plane and I'm more relaxed than I expect. I sit next to the captain, Matt Libby himself. We are shoulder to shoulder. There's a steering wheel (I'm sure there's a more technical name) projecting into my lap. I don't appreciate this because it implies, however remotely, that I might be expected to participate in the flying process in some proactive way.

The gear is loaded. Todd climbs in back. We wear headphones that allow us to hear Matt through a microphone. We push off from the dock in a casual way, as if we're just taking a quick trip in a motorboat. Before I know it, we're speeding down the lake and making a slow ascent into the north Maine sky. This feels like flying in a more analog way. We bank and can see the camp more clearly. It looks very peaceful and well considered. Beyond the lake are trees, everywhere trees.

It's more than just trees, of course. A river cuts all the way to the horizon, surrounded by remote ponds that looks like natural swimming pools. We circle one of the ponds and begin to descend. We head straight for it. For some reason my mind has not come to terms with the fact that there's no runway—the water's the runway. It's a gentle landing, we bump once or twice and then that's that. What could be easier?

We slow down and come to a stop at an island with a spartan log cabin up a hill and some green canoes on its bank. Libby Camps runs this cabin, if you want to spend the night even farther from civilization. It's empty now. Todd opens the door of the plane and steps down onto the pontoon. I note, with mild alarm, just how thin the door really is.

Then Matt pulls the plane to the shore. In its efficiency and logic, this is a great way to travel. We take out a small cooler, a dry bag, Todd's pack, my rod bag, and we're in business. Matt says he'll see us at four, as if he's dropping us off at school. He pulls away and takes off. We hear the plane after it's out of sight. Then the sound drifts away and it's quiet and feels very isolated.

A pond is manageable. You can see it at once and row across it. Trees line the entire banks. It's like a short story, you know the arc of the plot in one sitting. We're fishing out of an Old Town canoe. This is what Dave and I used in Wisconsin, though this one, at twenty feet, is longer. The company has made good canoes since around 1900, they used to be wood and canvas, then fiberglass, and now polyethylene. Polyethylene, in my experience, is both slightly pliant and indestructible. In fact, they're made not too far from here, in Old Town, Maine.

Todd rows from the back, the gear is in the center, I'm in the bow. Let's do this. If a pond seemed simple at first, now, when I'm deciding where to cast, it does not. We don't just move around the edge of it, there are hidden contours, and Todd knows them. The brook trout like the fall-offs where they can stay deep and safe but watch what swims overhead in case they want to come up and eat. I tie on a Caddis, a classic fly that looks a little like a dust broom, the size of a kernel of corn. If I was here on my own, I would have been at a loss, looking for rises or casting too close to the bank.

I'm enchanted by this arrangement. Float planes and remote ponds. It's both exotic and totally logical. Something about an isolated camp in the woods feels set in time and speaks to how few things we actually need. I've brought a wet bag with a water bottle, fly boxes, a rain jacket, and more nonsense than the men who built this camp would expect. It feels like we're alone in the world. A loon swims on the far shore.

Todd tells me that the best way to catch fish is probably with a streamer on a sinking line, which gives me pause. During this trip, I'm experimenting with some righteous dry fly purism. "Is there any way to start on top?" I ask. Todd obliges, he couldn't be nicer, in fact. I cast along the edge that he indicates. There are a few slow rises nearby, but nothing to my Caddis. As long as there's the occasional rise, I don't doubt my decision to stay on the surface. For the moment, at least, I'm patient. I don't feel the urgency I do when fishing in Montana. This seems more manageable. It's nice just to be in a canoe in this special place. It already feels like a victory.

I cast and let the fly drift. Well it's not a drift exactly, the fly floats, but there's not much of a current. In a pond, trout typically patrol a certain area—they don't stay in one place. So if one rises, you want to cast in front of it, since it's likely that it will keep moving. If they're not rising, however, then you have to be patient and watch your fly carefully. The trout can come from far down to take it, and this takes a few seconds. You might really have to let the fly sit there for a while. Then cast again. Then again. After a number of casts this feels a little redundant. In the middle of a pond you're not casting to a target. Todd brings us closer to some trees sunk in the water. That livens things up—it's good to have something to aim at. It's good to have variation.

What makes pond fishing great—its self-containment—

also defines its limitations when the fishing's slow. A pond is charming, but dropped off by an airplane, this is it. There's no plan B. Sitting in a pond casting is a little less dramatic than fishing on a river or on flats. We imagine fishing, and when we imagine it we always imagine catching fish. We don't think about what it's like with no fish. I know that ahead of time and embrace it.

I try to adopt this enlightened attitude, which just means I'm feeling impatient. I focus on the fact that I'm here for my pleasure. Fishing trips can get hijacked by expectations. You've planned, driven, and paid to get to some remote location, and by God man, you expect an agreeable trout every, say, twenty minutes. Well let's not be greedy, a trout every half hour. Just steady action and good fish—is that too much to ask? Yes, I'm afraid it is. Sometimes, rarely, you get the day of days, but not often, no matter how well you plan or how much you pray.

I keep this in mind as I continue casting and watch the Caddis sitting on the surface. I'm about to pick it up and cast yet again, when there's a rise. I raise the rod. This is my first trout in a canoe. A brook trout is strong and direct. It heads back down to the bottom of the pond. I strip in line. Now I can see the fish far below the boat, coming into focus against a deep green background, it's like looking down into space. The bottom of the pond seems completely endless, and the fish is in sharp relief. It looks even greener than the water. I strip in, the trout comes closer and I can see its blazing stomach. I lead it toward the back of the canoe, where Todd calmly nets it. "Never doubt the Caddis!" Todd says. When the equation works, nothing is simpler.

The fish is vivid and bright with vibrant yellow spots, as perfectly composed as a Dutch still life. It's probably about a foot long, a little less. Let's say a foot. The trout's old enough that the jaw is already pronounced. This is what we're dealing with here. There are larger fish in the pond, but this is more typical. It's lovely. Todd quickly lets it go, and, the drama over, the pond returns to its normal existence. Everything is in its right place at its right pace. The canoe continues along its path, forty feet from the shore.

We eat lunch on the bank beneath the old camp. It's nice to get out of the canoe and move around. When you're truly isolated you realize just how rare that is. The same way when you see a sky without the lights of a city, your life is thrown into some contrast. Matt's father found this pond. In the 1940s he realized that it would be easier to reach these ponds by flying float planes to them. So he bought a plane.

In the afternoon I catch a few more trout on the surface. Some are small and feisty for their size. The large ones are more deliberate, more stubborn and stronger. They just don't want to come to hand. Finally, we return to the bank and unload the canoe, and Todd flips it over near the others beneath a tree. At 4 p.m. we hear the float plane before we see it land and coast easily toward the bank.

We climb in and Matt asks how our day was.

"Terrific," I respond. "What a setting."

"That's good. I've always liked it here. I try to come to this camp every year."

We take off. I look down and across the landscape and wonder what it means to commit yourself to a place. I know that question can't be answered in the abstract.

A few years later I'm excited to return to Libby Camps. I'm in Portland with my friend Andrew, who owns a bar and restaurant here. The night before driving up we eat a steak ("the butcher's cut," he calls it) covered with a secret spice rub. He casually opens oysters bought from a woman at the farmers market. Eating oysters on the deck feels like a good advertisement for Portland. Andrew's steak, cooked over very low heat, is so good I seriously reassess my grilling skills.

Over the summer, I helped Andrew prepare for the trip. I sent him links to vintage wading boots (usually in the wee hours, when I'm on the lookout for such things). One of the joys for any trip is deciding what you need to properly outfit yourself. Is the old rain jacket good enough? (Probably, but better check eBay to make sure there's not an older one that might be even less good enough.) We inspect dry bags, old reels, new flies, waders, canvas rod cases, Wheatley fly boxes. The fact that most lodges offer rods and reels doesn't deter us. We need our own, as a matter of propriety. Some of this is to say that Andrew doesn't leave his family high and dry often to fish. This is a rare escape for him so we plan carefully.

We have a crucial visit on our itinerary. On Route 1 we arrive in Waldoboro and can see Moody's. But we turn left and drive west on a country road. We arrive at Morse's Sauerkraut, one of America's great establishments. That's

partly because of its improbability—a German delica-
tessen in remote Maine—but mostly because of its sheer
brilliance. It opened in 1918, and the sign calls it a "Euro-
pean Market." That may be true, but it feels more German
to me.

They sell house-made summer sausage, a careful selec-
tion of Rieslings, and half-sour pickles that may be the
world's best food that comes in a jar. There's a true deli
with your favorite wurst, whether that favorite is knock-
wurst, blutwurst, or bratwurst. And of course there's
kraut just like they've made since Virgil Morse's day, from
cabbages they grow themselves. There's more: tins of fish in
oil, brown mustard in ceramic jars made by French monks,
my beloved McVitie's biscuits. Oh, and there's a small restaurant where they serve this sort of food, and a schnitzel,
to boot. Who needs another lobster roll?

Andrew and I pack the cooler with Riesling, pickles,
and sauerkraut as if we're going to a picnic in Alsace. We
wind our way on small highways past farmhouses in vary-
ing stages of disrepair. The leaves get brighter. We stop at
a good vantage point of Mount Katahdin. We are being
pulled upward. We head due north.

I've warned Andrew about the road. Twenty miles of dirt
is an abstraction until you reach mile two, when reality sets
in. Trees line the road, their leaves yellow. Returning to
a place after a long absence, you reconstruct memories—
some things are vivid, some misremembered, some suddenly recalled. There's no old man at the gate. In his place

is a video camera and a sign that instructs me to pick up a phone and call a number. A woman answers and lets us through. She's perfectly nice, but the process lacks a personal touch. Apparently they don't have gate attendants anymore. I guess a gatekeeper at a wilderness is out of step with the times. I didn't realize anybody came here to be in step with the times.

We arrive at Libby Camps and head to our cabin. It's simply furnished. Two beds, two chairs, a stove, a table, and a surprising number of cribbage boards, apparently they're made nearby. This reminds me that the last time I played cribbage was in Maine, back in college. My friend and I played on my radio show, which we thought was transgressive or Dada or some combination of things. That may have been why we were on the air at 3 a.m.

I wake up at six, not my ideal time. The fact that we enjoyed some cognac last night makes it even less of an ideal time. The only reason I get up this early is to fish. Andrew is unbothered, he's already up building a fire in the stove. "I have two kids," he explains. "My internal alarm clock is set for five." I step onto the deck and look down where the lake should be. It's invisible, beneath heavy fog. A thin line of trees is faintly visible across on the far bank, like a charcoal drawing.

There's already a fire in the large stone fireplace in the lodge. Fire is a fact of life here, the original form of heat is all there is. The dining room is two stories high up to a pitched roof. There are mounted brook trout on the wall, along with about every animal in the area that can be killed with a shotgun. If I'm in Maine I feel like blueberry pancakes are in order, served with real Maine maple syrup—take that, Vermont! My feeling is vindicated.

We're fishing with Cole, a certified Maine guide. This is an important distinction, other states do not have this designation. To become a certified Maine guide you have to pass a test. You can be a hunting guide, fishing guide, or general outdoor expert. Cole is all three. Former navy, an expert caster, he can spot a grouse at any distance in record time.

Andrew and I head down to the dock with our rods, duffels, and various dry bags, feeling very prepared for anything that might come our way. As instructed, we're already in our waders and boots. What's surprising about float planes is just how small the cabin is, like getting into a Fiat. When I flew here before, it was with Matt, who's since retired. Now the camp is run by his son, Matt Jr., and he does the flying. Matt Jr. flies so much it's completely commonplace for him. Not us—we're excited. After one round trip the last time I was here, I now feel like a steely-eyed, battle-scarred float plane veteran. The plane pulls out onto the lake and gets louder before it picks up enough speed to start its slow rise. Suddenly everything is below us, the leaves vibrant with color. Orange, red, and green crossed decisively by a river. The plane lands in a lake, and we get out where it feeds into the mouth of a river.

Brook trout do not just live in ponds. They like pools in rivers, usually deeper ones. We drift dry flies, nymphs, and streamers through some of the best holes, and, after a very slow morning, Cole gets a little concerned. A guide has to have a balance. If a place is traditionally good, he can tell you in advance, then you focus more and work it carefully. The downside is if nothing happens then you know you're in a bad way. Or he can stay quiet and not tell you it's good. Then, after nothing happens, he might wistfully say, "That's usually a very good spot." Neither option appeals.

We kept coming to pools where fish should be, Cole didn't have to tell us that. We kept leaving without brook trout. He didn't have to tell us that either. We heard that there had been a drought, that the water was low. All the things you don't want to hear. It was getting tough. I wasn't just worrying about myself, I was worried about Andrew. This was a rare trip without his kids. He wasn't like Dave, who would rebound with a bonefish expedition.

Cole asks if we'd like to hear a poem. In a strong voice he recites a Western ballad, like a gothic Nick Cave song, his voice echoing back from the trees. We're impressed. I was not expecting this from Cole. There's an appealing touch of earnestness in his delivery. Excited by our enthusiastic reaction, he shares an off-color poem whose last line is "I bucked one and Tim bucked two," which is all you need to know.

We enjoy this side of Cole and trust that he's not trying to distract us from the travails of the river. Brook trout aren't supposed to make you work *this* hard. I turn to Cole, sport to guide, and ask, "So what do you think?" This is the time to speak freely. If the fishing is bad, it isn't Cole's fault. We're all in this together. "I don't know," he replies. "I'm not too happy about it." I wonder if he's trying to remember another poem.

Attentive to the plummeting morale, Cole points downstream and asks if I see the foam line. "Cast above it and let the fly run all the way through." I do as I'm told, cast and throw in a large upstream mend. The drift starts and, just as Cole foretold, the bobber plunges. I raise the rod. "Whoo-yeah!" Cole erupts. He lives part of the year in Arkansas, and his exclamation hints at a sort of adopted accent. We haven't seen this side of Cole. "Oh, that makes me so happy," he says. He's on a high. I laugh—I appreciate the enthusiasm, it mirrors emotions I'm keeping to myself. I still have to fight the fish. It tries to stay in the safety of the pool, but after a while, facing upstream, it tires. I lead the trout over to the shore; its color is visible before Cole nets it.

If you're alone when the fishing is slow it means one thing, and another if you're with a friend. If the trip was your idea and you came up with an entire scheme, you feel some responsibility, even though it's out of your control. This is complicated by the fact that I'm catching more of the fish. Spend enough time in a boat with another angler and you learn to respond when your friend catches more than you. On rare occasions the situation is reversed: Sometimes your friend struggles while you catch fish. Now, Andrew has a full life, a wife, two beautiful children, a dog, a business. He doesn't spend his time, like *some* people, fishing whenever he can. And it can be tough casting a sinking line out of a canoe, which is what we've done for a few days.

Andrew has an agreeable manner and is a natural host. He's tended bar during many of his adult years, so he's social, knows how to deal with people, is good with guides. He seems unbothered even though the first day was slow going. "I'm just happy to be here," he says. This is exactly what I want to hear, but I'm still slightly suspicious that he means it.

The second day, his casting monumentally improves, and Cole says so. This may be little consolation, because he's not getting rewarded for it. Andrew's doing the right thing, and I hope he knows that's enough. But do you want to be told you're doing the right thing or do you want to catch a fish? We all know the answer to that. This remains part of fishing—coming to terms with the fact that you can do everything correctly and still not receive deliverance. You can cast well, throw in a mend, let a drift go perfectly, and . . . nothing happens. Ideally everything aligns. Not always.

This exposes the myth that catching fish doesn't matter—sometimes you need to be rewarded. Not always, but sometimes, the loop needs to be completed. You need a rise, a set, a fight, and a trout. Action is part of the sport too. I try to focus on the positive. Having been in that position myself, having made every conceivable mistake and suffered shutouts, I feel uniquely positioned to cheer Andrew. The cognac that night does a more effective job than I do.

It's our last day. We're in the canoe on a long, narrow pond. Andrew is casting much farther than when we arrived, his movements more methodical, less hurried. I catch a nice trout in the morning and it feels like Andrew's turn. I can philosophize all I want and tell Andrew to take the long view, and make no mistake, I did. I'm sure I was an absolute bore. You just don't want your friend to return to civilian life and report that the fishing was appalling. I don't want that either because then he might not be able to fish with me again. It's very important to remain on good terms with the wives of your fishing friends. This is true for many reasons, but for the angler it's incredibly true because every fishing trip has to be run by her desk. Her veto power cannot be overridden.

That afternoon something changes. As happens after lunch and a beer, I lose a little focus. Not Andrew. He promptly catches a nice trout. He doesn't say *finally*, but he exhales in a way that indicates he can relax a bit. We all are at ease. The boat is happy. Andrew, naturally enough, but Cole just as much. I pass a beer up to Andrew. Everything finally aligns.

The sun shines down on us. *Sol Lucet Omnibus.* This was written on the blackboard of my seventh grade Latin class. On the first day, Mr. Schaefer pointed to those words and read them out loud: *Sol Lucet Omnibus.* "The sun shines on everyone." I forgot the conjugations and everything else, but I remember that. And the sun does shine down on us. The contour of the pond feels like the limit of our little world. And it's a complete world.

Andrew is a changed man. He promptly catches another fish. Great. Then another. Still great, possibly slightly less great, but only by degrees. Then another. Cole notes that amid this success one person in the boat is not catching anything. The philosophizer and morale booster of the morning is now at a loss. I'm fishless and speechless. I take a renewed interest in Andrew's streamer that looks like mine but is darker green. Cole feels comfortable enough to ask if I want the same fly. This is a time-honored, very friendly dig. I'm not too proud to ignore what's working.

Andrew is in the front of the canoe, which, let's admit it, is an advantage. There's wider casting range, you're the first to new water, and—I don't want to have to list all these things, so let's accept that sitting in the front of the canoe is an advantage. But this situation is no accident. Andrew lets his streamer sink much longer than I do. Cole is very clear on this matter: "You cannot let it sink long enough. The fish can be all the way at the bottom." I note his technique. Andrew strips at very specific intervals, two strips and a pause. I try to do it his way but still have the skunk on me. I had caught a few fish, but now it's just not happening.

When you're not catching fish in a pond, some of the charm goes out of the proceedings. In a river you're moving, whether you're on a boat or wading. You're covering water and working good lies. In a pond you're just in the pond. It's a clear day, no clouds, sun keeps the hatch away and the fish down. That means casting, letting it sink, then stripping in. That's not the traditional fly fishing equation of poetry and glory. Being in a canoe is also more passive than wading. On a drift boat at least you're standing.

Then Andrew's rod bends far down. A serious fish. This is getting out of hand. After a long fight, he hauls in a truly beautiful brook trout. The fish passes by me in the middle of the boat many times during this conflict. I'm getting a close-up look at what I wish was happening to me. Andrew is suddenly such a seasoned angler that, in his excitement, he wonders aloud if the fish is eighteen inches. I'm all for this new empowered version of Andrew, Andrew 2.0 angling phenom, but have to step in to tell him it's sixteen inches—which it is. That remains much larger than the fish I wasn't catching.

Variables matter. Depth, speed of line retrieval, also angle of retrieval. I was casting as far as I could every time and then stripping in at forty-five degrees instead of a shorter cast and pulling it more straight up from the bottom. In my state of shattered confidence I revisit all the truisms I shared with Andrew when he was struggling—*you did all you can do, it's about the complete experience, about more than catching fish*. This knowledge did not endear me to the situation. Andrew is too polite to rub it in, or even repeat my clichés back to me. If I was alone and not catching fish, I just would have thought it was an off day. Now I'm forced to confront the painful fact that the fishing is by no means tough for everyone. Cole chimes in: "Andrew, maybe you can give Dave here some advice." We all laugh, some harder than others.

When we make it back to camp, the sun is low in the sky and the warmth of the day is gone. We return to our cabin to find that the staff has already lit the stove. The heat when we open the door is very welcome. We clean up, then sit on the deck and look down at the lake and drink a bottle of Riesling from Morse's. Sometimes you feel like you're really in a place, that you appreciate its natural rhythms, the morning fog, the brilliant leaves, the evening light.

After dinner, Andrew and I go back to the cabin. I'm supposed to write something—yes it's absurd to try to work in this situation—but sometimes that's the price for disappearing from civilization. Andrew says it's fine. He opens the cognac, which is disappearing by our fourth night at an alarming rate. I don't feel like writing. I do like the look of the cognac. Andrew deserves to celebrate his day of triumph. I put the computer away—who was I kidding—and pour myself a glass.

"You did it," I say. "You caught the fish." Andrew laughs and shakes his head. We toast his brook trout. "Would you have had more fun yesterday if you knew you would have an amazing day today?" "I had a great time yesterday," he insists, "even when I wasn't catching anything, I was learning a lot." This is music to my ears.

"I have a question for you," Andrew asks. "If you were going to return, would you rather come back in June or September?" A new tradition, this is my language. I can tell by the flicker in his eye that Andrew's considering what he'll need on the next trip. "That's a good question." We have a long drive in the morning. There's plenty of time to discuss that on our way down to Portland.

ENGLAND

BROWN TROUT

Stealth

My apprenticeship was over. I had waited long enough. The time had come to go where it all started. To England. Yes, England! Where my beloved sport began, with its genteel traditions and unhurried pace. Chalk streams. Estates. Dukes in tweed. I was finally here to fish. I didn't want to get carried away, but it felt like I was here with a purpose.

It was like going to Montana for the first time. But when I went out West, I was a novice eager to learn. Fishing's pleasures and nuances were all in front of me. No longer. It was like returning to see Giotto's frescoes in Santa Croce after visiting them as a student. Now I was old enough to appreciate what was at stake. Fishing, naturally, means different things at different points in your life. I saved England until I was ready. As a confirmed obsessive, I wanted to come to terms with my place in the wider angling world.

They do things differently here. England maintains its own specific fishing customs. The rivers are not public. They're privately held or within estates, managed by outfitters who rent out stretches, about a mile long, called beats. There's nothing democratic about it, unless you consider paying for access democratic. If you meet the price of the landowner, you're on the water.

How did we arrive at this civilized place? In the 1800s, English gentry stocked brown trout in the water that flowed through their land. These weren't native fish. Once arrived, however, they thrived in the chalk streams full of the cool water trout enjoy and the insects trout *really* enjoy. The water was clear, and the trout, with plenty to eat, lived large.

To easily access the streams the English mowed pathways along their banks. They might put a bench in a particularly good setting, where they could light a pipe, contemplate the position, and look for rising fish. In the great good days, they would cast from the bank, in their country clothes, with a bamboo rod. The mowed banks are still there, the benches are still there, and at English outfitting stores the tweeds, corduroys, and tattersall are all still there.

There's more: You don't fish any way you want to. As in a Pall Mall club, there are rules, customs, ways things are simply done. During the height of the season, when the mayflies hatch—large green joyous insects—anglers cast dry flies upstream to rising trout. That's it. If the hatch is off, there's no nymphing, nothing subsurface, and certainly nothing as vulgar as a streamer. We're all gentlefolk here! This is sporting in the sense that it's challenging. Nymphing is frowned upon but allowed, or at least mildly tolerated, at the end of June, when the hatches are over and the fish feed near the bottom. Then, and only then, the angler can compromise and head down with a fly to meet the trout where they are.

That's not to say there's no nod to pleasure. On each beat is a small wooden hut with a table and a few chairs adorned with nothing (like a sauna) or quite a lot (kettle, wineglasses, a book with photos of people catching fish larger than yours). This hut, regardless of state of neglect, conveys a welcome sense of repose. We're here for a day outside, we endeavor to catch a trout, but we might also take a break for tea or a wee dram, and then begin our endeavor yet again. The hut implies a slower pace and, in its way, enforces it. This might not be how Americans imagine fishing. It's somewhat like a country walk beside a chalk stream. The fishing can even seem incidental. But fishing, of course, is never incidental.

So here I am, in England. It's late July. I had planned to come during the peak season, which begins in the middle of

May and runs for a month or so. That trip was postponed. Apparently, some things are more important than angling. It was hard to admit that, and even harder to re-book a trip when the best fishing days were behind me. I tried to be philosophical—I would be here when I would be here. Being philosophical often means pretending I'm not as mad as I actually am. Some fishing, however compromised, is certainly better than no fishing. But once I arrive, then I want better fishing. This is true of all anglers. I don't make the rules. It's just a fact.

I turn on BBC the morning of my big day. "Rain is expected today across the UK," the announcer intones, her positive voice straining, at odds with the forecast. I hear an echo of James Joyce's "The Dead": "Rain was general all over England." Rain is not surprising, though five countries under cloud seems excessive. I've been in the countryside two weeks, however, and every day was warm and sunny. It was eerie. The locals were cheered—they took walks, they tended gardens, they rode horses. It was all very English. They beamed at their good fortune. Not me. I watched this unfold with a growing feeling of dread.

Anglers obsess over weather, over *conditions*. We want the best chance to catch fish, naturally, but if it all goes south then *tough conditions* is the excuse nearest at hand. How was the fishing? *Well, conditions were tough out there.* That sounds vaguely scientific, the angler's specialty. The fact that we took it on the chin is conveniently not our fault. You can't argue with the weather.

Driving to the river as the sky darkens, I feel a sense of

misgiving. Certain English settings make me self-aware. Suddenly, I'm sensitive about my accent and the fact that I don't have a hyphenated last name. The English have a way of bringing this out in Americans. This is true even, perhaps particularly, of those with Anglophile tendencies, a group of which I count myself a casual member. It's not that we disapprove of the conventions—maybe we want to be accepted to the club, more than we'd like to admit.

Fishing in England doesn't happen by chance. You don't decide you're in the mood and stroll down to the water. If the weather's bad, you don't turn back. You reserve a section of a river and pay for it, usually long in advance. My dates were written in my calendar, in ink. As they drew near, I actually hoped for rain. A certain amount would help the water levels and cool down the streams, as trout are known to dislike low, warm water. But I really wanted rain because the obscure laws of angling mandated that when I finally fished in England, it would be in the middle of a storm. After weeks of sun, as I foretold, the sky opened the morning I arrived on the river.

This is the odd symmetry of the sport. You buy theater tickets months in advance knowing whichever day you choose will conflict with some urgent invitation. Likewise, your carefully planned fishing trip will coincide with a heat wave or pressure system or some other act of God that conspires to keep angler and fish apart. I've resorted to studying lunar cycles, hurricane histories, and weather almanacs. It never works. Now I give in to chance, point at the calendar, and throw a dart with the knowledge that I'm courting meteorological disaster.

I'm here for brown trout. Brown trout are everything, the benchmark, what we all aspire to. They're the most discriminating trout and, naturally, anglers being masochists, the most sought after. By discriminating, I mean the hardest to catch. If you caught one, Dave used to tell me, you knew there were ten more that you didn't catch. The brown trout is a fish worthy of being pursued by a gentleman, which is why the English used to wear ties to catch them. It was a sign of respect.

That's where the agreement ends. Never trust anybody talking about brown trout. We can't even agree about what color they are, except that they're not really brown. A brown trout is near black along the top, with a deep gold flank covered with vivid black, silver, and red spots. No two brown trout have the same pattern of spots. Each one is truly unique. Each one is a marvel.

Brown trout lead anglers into territory where emotion overwhelms judgment. The big fish come out at night, the truly large fish exist in stories. Nobody sees them. They're specters that possess the imagination of every angler, legends passing like state secrets. They start out *I'm serious*, to reassure the audience. *It was twenty-four inches.* Start the eye rolling. *No*, the angler insists, *it's true*. He wants you to trust a story that he would never believe from you. People who've lost the brown trout of their dreams remember every traumatic detail, and recount it dazed, as if staring unblinkingly into an eclipse.

Kingsley Amis said that a Macallan is the best thing you can put in a glass. You may disagree, but you know what he means. The brown trout is like that: It's the best thing you can take out of a river. Guides know this. When you miss a fish, from Idaho to Chile, the guide will wait a minute out of respect and say quietly, "Think it was a brown." A gloomy silence descends over the boat. The fact that the fish was never seen makes it even more painful, its potential size soaring since it escaped. It might have been the beast, the all-timer, the fish of fishes. *I felt it, and I swear to you, it was like a log.*

Rainbow trout don't have a care in the world. They're eager to eat, jump in the air, and come to hand. Not brown trout. They're finicky and judgmental, they brood. If you finally get a good one on the line, it will head down toward the bottom, it won't give you the pleasure of seeing it. Perhaps they're modest, but then you have to guess at their size, something anglers can't be trusted to do accurately.

Brown trout are a worthy pursuit and a fierce challenge. There are direct pleasures in angling, and one of them is catching a brown trout on the surface, to come up and take a fly in plain sight. For me, it remains a pinnacle of the sport. That's why I came to England.

Fishing is anticipation. That's the key element, which never ends. It happens with each cast. Then there's the broader anticipation when arriving in a storied setting. You make it to the English chalk streams and ask what you bring to this special place. It's a dangerous proposition to test yourself, there are so many ways to be disappointed. And fishing in the July heat, even more ways. The water's low and there's no real hatch. Do you appreciate the way I'm setting this up? Laying out the *tough conditions* right at the top. I tried to manage my own expectations. I laid down the pounds, I reserved my beats, I hired a guide.

I'm going to meet my guide in a parking lot near the River Allen. A parking lot? That doesn't exactly sound idyllic. I'm eager to come face-to-face with an English guide, a figure of some romance in my imagination. Tony is standing on the side of the road. From a distance I think I'm having a vision, he looks like a cross between Tom Stoppard and Jimmy Page. This is a good sign since Tom Stoppard is my hero and ideal fishing partner (something he practices well), and English rock royalty often adopt the sport as they spend their silver years in grand estates like bloodline royalty. Tony has immense wavy pepper-and-salt hair and a broad, welcoming smile. He's expertly rolling a cigarette, and has the face and voice of a man who's done that many times a day, for many years. He's disarming; this is a man you want to fish with, to talk late into the night with. Here's a man I can do business with.

I pull on waders and put on a raincoat for the storm. I'm a waterproofed version of myself. The Allen is the rare English river where wading is permitted—more rules!— generally they want you out of the water, on the banks, not disturbing the stream. If I imagined a country stroll in corduroy and moleskin, this is not it. Tony puts on a black-brimmed hat clearly worn many times. He looks like a member of an aging, if still successful, band. He studied art at Winchester, a nearby town. "Where Brian Eno attended uni," he notes with a small amount of pride.

English guides spot fish, discuss tactics, and keep up morale. I'll need all of Tony's skills because we both know the fishing will be hard. Tony diverts me with a series of brilliant stories. "Where there's tea, there's trout," he observes. "The English and Scots grew tea and they brought their fish with them." This is a concise miniature history I appreciate. Tony can also be instructive on historical and geographical matters. "That's where the Vikings cut across the country, and first they struggled in the mud," he explains. "But then they did what Vikings do." Tony raises an eyebrow. I'm flattered by his presumption that I know what Vikings did. As an American my history gets hazy by the year 1066. I imagine he means pillaging, dominating, wreaking havoc, taking property by strife. I don't mention that my American football team is also called the Vikings. They try to do what Vikings do, except they lose every Super Bowl they play in.

Tony guides for salmon in Scotland and possesses a respectful appreciation toward the difficulty of that pursuit. "In salmon fishing you have one chance a day, and if you're good enough," he says, "you'll know you've missed it." I smile at this aphorism's turn until I realize it might have some bearing on my episode with the phantom knock in Canada. I quickly banish it from my mind. Tony is also an expert on relatively exotic tactics. I compliment him on one cast he shows me. He shrugs it off. "It's a bit like being good at snooker," he replies. "The sign of a misspent youth."

His charm is the antidote to the storm. But the storm comes anyway. Tony, to his credit, is honest enough to look at the sky and sigh. Nobody wants to be the first to concede we're in a bad way. We both know it's going to be tough. If we had our choice, we would ditch today and come back tomorrow. We're already on the books. The check has been cashed. Now is the time.

The River Allen is barely visible from the road. I follow Tony through a gate and we drop my gear—more than a gentleman would need—at the small hut. Branches obscure the narrow stream. When we finally get a good look I see that it's narrow, the width of a country lane. The water is on our left, a farmer's field on our right, trees blow lazily in the distance, indifferent to the weather.

We stand at the beginning of the beat on the banks of this thread of water. It's 9 a.m. The River Allen is rather obscure, with the character and intimacy of a stream. A river holds more secrets, is wider and more unknowable. Perhaps a stream is unknowable too, but it offers the illusion of understanding. This gives me a small amount of confidence, the fish should be easier to find. But the signs are not in my favor. *Conditions are tough.*

"You see that patch of green?" Tony asks as we walk down the beat. He must know the answer because I'm gazing despondently at the runway of weeds waving gently down the middle of the stream. I have the dazed look of somebody holding twenty when the dealer pulls black-jack. "Yes," I reply, more sharply than I intended. It's less a patch of green, really, more a swath. Even a wide swath, an *imposing swath*, of green. "Now that would not be here earlier in the season," Tony concludes, gently placing a dagger in my back. A dense runway of algae running like a traffic jam down the middle of the stream is not what you want to see, not what you want to hear about, and, most crucially, not what you want to cast over. The line will get caught up in the weeds and make drifting beyond it nearly impossible. Another bad sign.

Earlier that week, during the days of sunshine and mirth, I bought a book, *Trout Fishing*, published in 1943. The author, one H. D. Turing, claimed the sport will take the aspiring angler "into the realms of unfettered enjoyment." Well that sounded very civilized and nice. I like enjoyment, and ideally I prefer my enjoyment to be unfettered. But fishing rarely leaves those realms unfettered, more likely they are slightly fettered. And if there are weeds across half the river then the enjoyment is very bloody fettered indeed.

I try to adopt a philosophical approach. I finally made it to England. Naturally, it's the wrong time of year. More naturally, the state of the river, which isn't really a river, is awful. More naturally still, the conditions are appalling. But that's all right. Let's see what happens. Fishing owes me nothing. The world moves as the world moves. Sometimes you're blessed and catch a perfect brown trout. Other times you catch about eighteen overhanging branches and it's nearly impossible to cast and within an hour you think, *Good Lord, what was I thinking coming here in July?*

After an hour of trying to get a cast over a fish and catching yet another branch, I have some strong words for my situation. I consider technical fishing to be about precise casting, careful mending, and long drifts on fine tippets. This is not that. I can barely get the line onto the water. With the obstructions, casting is so difficult I may have raised my temper. One of the participants may have said that the situation was a shit show. That participant may have been me. Tony smiles at this undignified behavior. "Don't beat yourself up," he says kindly. "You have to have a sense of humor on a day like today."

Tony is right and I appreciate his sentiment—and adopt it. That lasts about five minutes. I did not come here to laugh, I came here to catch trout. We spot a trout, and it flees as soon as I begin to move my rod. "It could detect your intentions," Tony notes drily, and breaks into a deep, tobacco-infused laugh. What else can I do? I have to laugh too.

Our *Trout Fishing* author moved on from the enjoyments of angling into more critical waters. He warns of the "false purist who is apt to claim superiority for his method simply because he knows no other and covers the meagreness of his attainments." Well, H.D., I don't want to take this personally, but whose *meagre attainments* would you be referring to? He wasn't done. "Such men can at times be decidedly trying." For a book on the joys of fishing, this seemed like a personal takedown. Feelings were getting hurt.

I think of this as I stand with Tony, staring at the river. He recalls a story, like many of his stories told many times and better for it. It is of a day when he was struggling to catch trout on dry flies, which he refused to change, on principle. "My puritanism came back to bite me in the ass," he says. "And not for the last time." The moral is clear: We will not be so pure that we'll insist on catching a trout on the surface if they're feeding on the bottom.

So we won't use dry flies, whether or not it's my pinnacle of the sport. That's not in the cards. I tie on a very small nymph. "If they see it and want it," Tony reassures me, "they'll take it." That makes it sound like a fairly straightforward proposition. But to even get to that point we have to get in a position where I can make a cast—close enough to a trout but not so close I spook him. That's the exact push and pull that makes fishing wonderful in theory and excruciating in practice.

This challenging fishing benefits from experience in the field. But you can't easily replicate overhangs, banks of reeds, ripping wind, and spooky fish. You just have to live through them. We aren't even using strike indicators—the shadow of a small bobber might frighten the trout. So, yes, it's a pain. You come to England to cast a large mayfly the size of a bottle cap with trout crashing the surface. We're here fishing a nymph we can't see. But it's the only game in town.

Now, I have no problem casting to fish and not catching them. In fact, I enjoy it. Each cast, each drift, is a possibility. After a certain amount of time you decide if you want to change your approach. This, I would submit, is a great part of fishing. It's the time-honored friction between Carter's tactical changes and Dave's insistence on holding the line.

What I'm doing on the River Allen is very different. Forget drifting over trout, I can barely get a cast into the narrow lanes of water that aren't obscured by overgrown branches or full of weeds. When there's an open lane with a fish holding, I catch something on the back cast, a branch I haven't seen. "Where the hell did that tree come from?" is not something you want to hear yourself saying.

We walk a mile, through the entire beat, and I manage to get a drift over one disinterested trout, maybe two. I feel like anglers shouldn't be allowed on this river that's barely a river. Then I think of my friend Markley. He loves this type of challenging fishing. The more archaic and unconventional the casting, the better. Backhand casts, sidearm casts, highly accurate roll casts—it doesn't have to be pretty, just figure out a way to get your fly on the water. Why should a river keeper trim branches and reeds to make it easier for the vanity of certain casting-challenged anglers?

Tony and I regroup at the hut. Everybody draws the line somewhere. I think of my friends who are purists, who use dry flies, and only dry flies, no matter what the trout are doing. Usually these strong believers have a habit of reminding you of their faith. On the other end of the spectrum is my good friend Matt, who likes to catch fish any way he can. Once he fished all day on an English river to limited effect. Late in the afternoon, and very much in private, he tied on a streamer and stripped it through a few deep holes. This is frowned upon the way that burning a Bible in the Vatican is frowned upon. It's beyond not done, it's heresy.

A streamer is large, weighted, and, when retrieved quickly, resembles a minnow and instigates large, wary trout. It's instinctive. It doesn't require much finesse. Dragging a streamer through a pool of fish that has never seen one is like bringing a keg and a stack of red Solo cups to a freshman dorm—it will draw attention and use. The results for Matt? You might have guessed: He caught two fish in as many casts, both quite large. As he strode away from the stream, before he might be reprimanded and banned, rather than be weighed down by any sense of guilt, he felt pretty good about it. He told the story as a success, even a triumph of American ingenuity, a revelation of what we all actually want but are afraid to admit. I envy Matt's direct pursuit of action even at the expense of tradition.

This is a slippery slope. First you use a dry fly and that doesn't work, then you try the nymph. No action? Then a nymph with another nymph trailing behind it. That isn't getting it done. Do you try a streamer? If that doesn't work, where does it end? Using bait? *Bait for goodness' sake! Heathenish, soul-destroying bait! Would you fish with a worm, a live worm, just for the action?! Good grief, get ahold of yourself, man!*

What are we all doing here: trying to prove a point or trying to catch a fish? That's a question for all time. The fly angler is already asking, If it's easy, is it worth doing? Well, I want to catch a trout the right way and the hard way. Then, after a fair amount of suffering, I want to catch one a slightly less noble way, and so on. That progression, and the patience required, varies for every angler. It's even different for the same angler at different points in his life.

We still go through our progressions. At the bottom of this list is the Woolly Bugger. The Woolly Bugger is effective and possibly evil, the last chance and maybe the best chance. It looks like a furry black caterpillar, and if you pull a Woolly Bugger through a pool, a trout will come take a look and, especially if the trout hasn't seen one, probably take it. There's a store in the Catskills that refuses to even sell Woolly Buggers. They represent either true desperation or canny tactics. Catching a trout on a Woolly Bugger is shedding your principles, it's winning ugly.

Is this discussion minor, is it overthought? You know it is! But fly fishing reflects the values of its practitioner and this remains a central issue. Essentially, how you want to catch a fish. Do you prize artistry or results? You learn about yourself over time, you become more patient or less, more discerning or less. But England doesn't let you express your own theories, England imposes its own rules. One of England's first rules is no Woolly Buggers. And, unless you're like Matt, and sneak in streamers, you will fish the traditional way, laid down by the men who invented the sport. There's a code here, and you measure yourself against that code. So where did it end in England? I didn't know yet, but it didn't look good.

My head swirls. Until something good happens, I focus on the bad things. What runs through my head is not a Taoist phrase or the sound of one hand clapping. It's the repeated and insistent words, a mantra at my own expense: *Don't get shut out.* Getting shut out might be called character building—at a certain age your character is built enough. It could also be called morale shattering, a fool's errand, an epic failure, or a total waste of time. Everything collapses as you look for some larger meaning. I'm all for angling enlightenment, but getting shut out is never a good option. I'm afraid it might become a reality.

Stay calm, I tell myself, a lot can happen. Even though everything that happened on the water suggested complete and total devastation. I'm an optimist, right? Toward the end of the morning the rain finally lets up, and now it's easier to see the trout. We are next to a wider pool in front of a small bench. Some of the best places to fish in England have little benches on the bank. That's a clue that people have spent time there looking for and then casting to rising fish. These are wider, deeper pools in slightly larger clearings. Mere angling mortals can actually make a cast.

There are fish in these pools, in places trout should be. It isn't secret, they just aren't feeding. A feeding fish stays in its lane, facing upstream, and slightly turns its head to take nymphs floating toward him. Trout that aren't feeding move more haphazardly. They're distracted and paranoid. A feeding fish is focused.

And a feeding fish is what we finally find. I cast the nymph in front of it. A short cast, with no drama or excess motion. I manage to avoid trees behind me on either side. It's an unromantic cast, according to images of the sport, but what's called for in the moment. It serves a purpose, something fast and practical, like a colloquial phrase in French, which I struggle with in fishing and in French. The nymph falls in the water just above the fish and begins to sink. Remember, there's no bobber, we're doing this all by sight, on a day without a lot of light. I can barely make out the subtle move of the trout's head, but I briefly see a clear, impossibly thin sliver of white—the inside of its mouth. It's eaten something, I think it's my nymph but can't believe it, that would be too easy. And so far nothing has been easy.

I raise my rod and, after a second I can only describe as excruciating, feel the pressure of a good trout on the line. In case I'm hallucinating, I hear Tony. "Well done," he bellows. "Well done, indeed." I still have to fight the fish—I'm not sure why Tony thinks landing it is a foregone conclusion. The pool isn't big, which amplifies the disturbance; the calm of the day is interrupted. Catching a fish in a small pool brings a vivid amount of drama to an enclosed space. The trout can't go far up- or downstream, so he goes down to the bottom until he tires out or you have the confidence to raise him to the net. After a few dives I feel the fish is under control. Tony dips his net in the river. When he raises it, there's a brown trout that's big enough to thrill me. I'm not embarrassed to say I grin like a schoolboy. "It's a simple sport," I say. And in that moment it is. All the thinking is gone, and a brown trout, vivid even under the gray sky, remains. The red spots seem redder, but they always do. Like all brown trout, it is like no other.

Now we can eat lunch in peace. Lunch when you've been shut out can be a bit testy. There's too much time to think about the horribleness of the fishing. After a late morning fish it's quite festive. Beer after you've caught a fish tastes monumentally better than beer when you haven't caught a fish—that's basic science. I also look forward to a pork pie with pickle chutney I brought, which feels very decadent. This sense of indulgence is increased when Tony dispatches two Scotch eggs, a heroic feat, as if it's the most natural thing in the world.

England is good at this sort of meal. Here's my personal (but definitive) list of portable English food:

- *McVitie's Dark Chocolate Digestives.* You shouldn't eat food that comes in a package. You know this. If you do eat food from a package, then it should be McVitie's, which rival Snyder's pretzels for between-meal supremacy. These are wheat biscuits that are the exact right amount of biscuit-i-ness and dark chocolate that's not at all sweet, and very addictive. An acceptable substitute for breakfast but good at any time of day.
- *Pork Pie.* Preferably from a good butcher. This is something that you're glad doesn't come with any sort of nutritional information because it would blow off the page. You could not eat for two days afterward and still gain weight. The pork pie with its baked crust is the size of a small hockey puck, and can lay low anybody. Enjoy with a sweet chutney, like Branston pickle, for maximum effect.
- *Sausage Roll.* Pastry around ground sausage. Should probably be illegal, and the fact that it is rarely found outside the UK indicates that it might well be. Best eaten in private.
- *Fish & Chips.* Not *that* portable. I order this at the

first pub I'm at because *I'm in England*. And then
the second one the next day to compare. The third
one is for science. And the fourth, as A. J. Liebling
might say, is for symmetry.
- *Pint of Bitter.* I want to be the type of person who
likes bitter, ale, and the rest of it. I have yet to arrive
at that hallowed ground, though not without trying.

"Why are you ordering that again?" a loved one asks.
"Because I want to make sure I don't like it."
"You are sure."
"Am I?"
I am.

That night I stay at the Compasses, a seventeenth-century
pub. It's on a road that, I am told, the Romans used. Oh
right, the Romans. Don't forget about the Romans. The
building is white plaster with timbers and a thatched roof.
It's what I want from a pub. A large fireplace all the way up
to the ceiling. I like fireplaces, especially when I can enter
them standing up. The rest of the room is devoted to a small
bar and tables.

People from the area come by with their dogs, their
ancient Land Rovers, and all seem to know one another.
The pub offers to buy vegetables from anybody in the area
who grows them. They'll add them to the menu, which is
very civilized. It feels like the right place to be. In case I
think this place was living in the past, the bartender has
painted his fingernails a handsome shade of blue. The next

morning I have a startlingly good breakfast of scrambled eggs and salmon. Toast arrives in one of those silver vertical holders, with butter from a nearby dairy and jam so dark you know it's made right there. The sky is clear. The weather has moved out.

Over the next few days, Tony and I establish a routine that I come to associate with English fishing. We walk downstream the length of the beat, slowly enough that we can see where the fish lay. When we make it to the bottom, we walk back up and try to cast to those fish. When we finally reach the top, we're at the hut and have tea while Tony rolls a perfect cigarette. It's nice. Each time through the beat we get to know it better. After three or four times, with lunch in between, you are fishing in England.

Yet all was not arcadian. Planes fly overhead on their way to Heathrow, trains speed by on obscured tracks, intruding at high volume onto our idyll. One river, in the backyard of a manor house, backs up onto the owner's par-3 golf hole. It's a storied stream but feels like a rich man's folly. My English ideal is coming into contact, if not conflict, with the reality of it, like finding out Cary Grant's real name was Archibald Leach. But the reality is supposed to be good enough because it's more human. It's great to dream of England, but there's no golf in my dreams. And it never rains in my imagination.

One morning, before heading out for the day, I stop by the market to buy beer (which, in England comes in a four-pack). I discover that you can't buy beer in England before

9 a.m. This provides a sense of symmetry to the first time I learned the same thing in Montana. The lessons are still coming.

The weather holds. Heat wore on us as we fished the River Nadder, which flowed easily beside sheep meadows. These sheep were recently shorn, marked with a blue number on their backside, identifying their flock. They had sweet round faces and were quite shy. I cast from a raised bank above the water, a slight disadvantage, particularly on sunny days, because the angler and his shadow are more visible to fish, which feel particularly vulnerable. Trout prefer to be hidden from birds, their predators come from above. How do you know if a fish sees you, your rod, or your line? Well, while you're wondering if they do, they dart away and settle the matter.

Serious anglers talk about stealthy approaches to clear streams. I should be stealthier, but then get excited and want to look for fish. This is a bad habit and I need to be more disciplined. Nick Lyons, in his wonderful book *Spring Creek*, describes casting from a sitting position a good distance from the water—he didn't even walk up to the stream. That sounds drastic until you look out from behind a tree, swear you're being discreet, then feel your heart sink as a twenty-inch fish dips away from under the bank.

In England the fish were so beautiful. Most of the time they weren't rising. That was the problem. They were down in the water column. That was another problem. They were spooky, a third problem. I was losing my casting edge, a fourth. We fished the entire beat with nothing to show for it and were back at the shed. If I'd had a flask, I would have referred to it.

I tried to see the bigger picture. I made some good drifts but nothing happened. It's all you can do. I would have cast again at some of these trout and worked them more intently. Tony did not agree. "The first chance is by far the best chance," he counseled. In essence, if you didn't get it on your first drift, or maybe your second, then move on. But if I drifted a nymph right past, and I mean right past, the nose of a fish and it did nothing, maybe I should try another nymph or maybe try something else. "Let's let the pool rest," Tony said tactfully. "We'll be back here." I would have to wait to try my luck again.

It's the last day. Tony pulls off a fairly well-traveled high-way and suddenly we're surrounded by trees. His jeep smells like stale smoke. We park and walk down a path not too far from the road, but it feels far. We are going to a special place, and it feels farther from the world than it is. This is the River Test. Legendary water. We arrive at a hut, but this hut is different than the others. It has a kettle, wine-glasses, charcoal, a shelf with some books. It's elegant in a rustic way. Everything suggests anglers are going to have a memorable day here. It even has a Weber outside—the grill that's one of the great American inventions. Maybe this is a sign. The fact that I'm even thinking this way reveals my desperate search for cosmic intervention.

We head down to the bank, just as we've started every other day. Again, the water isn't too far across. Again, the river has a peaceful, unassuming manner. It feels like an old place, and that walking beside the water should feel like enough. You could be here and need nothing else. Well, you would need a fishing rod. There are fish near the bottom of the stream, the largest we've seen, large enough to make my knees weak.

The hut where we arrive is at the bottom of the beat, so we head upstream and fish as we go. From the path I can only attempt backhanded casts and it's difficult going, another jab against left-handers. The fish are disinterested. We cross the river on a narrow bridge, and now I can cast from my natural forehand side. What's this? Fish are rising. I haven't seen steadily rising fish my entire time here. It's a miracle. A feeding fish is unsuspecting—it's focused on food—which makes it easier to do what you need to do. What they're eating is impossible to tell, the flies are so small.

I observe this surreptitiously from behind a bank of reeds. The sun is on my back and I feel the heat, luckily my shadow doesn't fall onto the water. Tony stands back and gives me space. This is what I came here for, what I dream of doing anywhere: casting to rising fish. So I cast to them. They're open-minded. They inspect my fly. Sometimes with intense curiosity, sometimes with vague interest, most of the time with utter indifference. I do not move on. I do not let the pool rest. I work through my fly box and cast to these fish for thirty minutes, changing my rigs and leaders and flies. Carter would have been proud of the tactics if not the results.

I know this is not Tony's strategy, but at this moment

it's mine. The fish don't mind. They're still rising. I've gone through five flies and countless drifts. It's not a glorious episode. It has an air of desperation. But it's fun—I feel like I have a chance—which is really all I want. And it reminds me of a personal angling philosophy: You're one cast away from being a genius. Catching a fish justifies your tactics and makes your path seem inevitable, even downright heroic. Still, I don't feel too smart at the moment, though I think that might change.

I choose the smallest fly I have from my emergency small fly box, something I never use. I don't even know the name of the fly, and in the heat I struggle to tie it on. I cast it nearly right on top of a fish that turns its head and in one motion takes it off the surface. This is a little fly, the size of half a chocolate chip, the size of a child's fingernail, the size of a crumble of stale bread. Am I making myself clear? The fly is small. The trout, however, is big. A lot can go wrong. It's hard to hook a large trout on a little fly and harder to land it. You can't pressure him quite as much. So I raise the rod, and blessings on us all, that little fly is flush in the trout's mouth. I did it my way.

The trout goes down toward the bottom, the other fish in the pool are now worked up and dart around. Then it swims upstream—this is a much longer pool and he has room to go. The current is slow and I don't worry about losing control of him. Finally he tires and I bring him near the bank. Tony roars, and comes over with his net, and we land a lengthy brown trout. On the bank, its silver side shines in the sun. We return him to the water and he sits on the bottom of the pool. Then Tony and I walk down to the hut again. The heat of the day is upon us and the trout will take their siesta. We caught it just in time.

The afternoon heat subsides, and finally its last licks on the River Test. I feel the nervous energy that comes at the end of a fishing trip. There's an hour left, the light gets softer. The book gets thinner, the last page nearer. Have you read a novel and tried to decide if the hero will survive? Did you turn ahead to find out what happens?

The end of a trip is a time of gratitude and bittersweet desire. You fish for days, but what happens in the last hour gives those days its shape. This is a dangerous business. It brings too much importance to what's supposed to be a diversion. Sometimes you need a diversion from the diversion.

Fish are rising as it's time to go, as if they're reminding me what they do in season: *This is why people come here, Yankee, thanks for visiting!* There's a group of brown trout, leisurely taking flies from the slow-moving surface of the river. The difference from earlier in the day is remarkable. Now they're rising, unhurried and languorous, unbothered and stylish.

Normally, we won't cast to fish that we walk by, they'll be too unsettled. Tony rolls another cigarette and nods. Give it a chance. This is still technical. I have no illusions. We can't see the fly they're taking. I don't mean we can't tell what it is: We literally can't see the damn thing. It's like a blue-winged olive but lighter, almost white. Tony and I keep using whatever flies in our boxes most resemble wisps of fluff. Sometimes the trout look at the fly or they follow it curiously. Other times they come up against it with an excruciating slowness, pushing the surface of the water up, literally nose the fly, and turn back down, leaving my legs shaking.

Forget all that. It's all about to end. I make an unusually accurate backhanded cast, the rare cast I'd like to be associated with. A brown trout turns and takes the small fly without hesitation. I set the hook, the fish heads as deep as it can before finally surfacing when it's netted by Tony, who has returned to my side. I can't believe it. "That never happens," I say. He knows what I mean. "Four days of that and you'd have been tired of it," he replies. I know what he means. I laugh and try to decide if I agree with him. Could I ever tire of casting to rising trout in the last light of a summer evening? We walk back toward the hut in the shadows along the bank and I think I know the answer.

AFTERWORD

HOME WATER

Travel is the ideal, though it remains the exception not the rule. Most of my fishing is done on a small stream in upstate New York, a few hours from where I live. The stream has the character of a mountain brook as it flows through a meadow, over dramatic falls, and down through a narrow gorge into a valley. This is my favorite place to fish.

There are rhythms to the year. In April, the water is

brisk and high with runoff. Surprise snowstorms arrive then turn to rain. The trout are reluctant, and that's all right, it's just nice to come into the season. Every day the hills in the valley turn greener, we pull ramps from the ground, and the fishing picks up. In summer the water goes down, the afternoons become warm, and the trout are in their element, feeding, relaxed, even playful. The sun sets late and the fireflies come out. By fall, the fishing slows and being on the water as the leaves change color is its own pleasure. The season is ending with fires in the fireplace. Every trout feels like it's the last of the year, and you count the days you still have on the water.

I know I'll return to this stream, so there's less urgency. The fishing varies, as it does everywhere and I can appreciate what's out of my control. I still try to improve, still try to learn. What works one day is comically ineffective the next. The more you're on a stream the more you realize how much there is to know. I take a longer view, there's no other way. The fishing is broader than the days, they add up and become part of a life.

I put too much emphasis on fishing—giving in to the obsession is one of angling's rewards. I think about fishing before I'm on the water and afterward, in that sense it never ends. There's a different meaning in the moment you connect with a fish, action replaces theory, analysis makes way for drama. This is not speculation or a wistful memory—it's completely in the present tense, the stream forms the contour of my world. All of this, taken together, is the sport, which, when you love it, is more than a sport.

I still try to get closer to an honest feeling of being connected to the world and of my place in it. This happens when I look at paintings made by monks, long dead, who believed in things I do not believe in. It happens, in the best moments, when I'm fishing. I fish for the contained and enduring pleasures of the sport, but also to escape the disappointments of modern life. In their place, for a short time, is a feeling of recognition, of being more human than at other times, of knowing the burden and thrill of being alive.

Fly fishing has taken me to a part of a heightened world. I knew something changed when I began dreaming of fish. In the dreams I look for trout and am excited when I find one. They say you can't see your hands in dreams, and I never see mine. But I cast, not knowing what will happen. In the waking life I cast too, and still I never know. If no trout rises, I cast again. I feel a shiver of good fortune to be in the world, a world without end.

ACKNOWLEDGMENTS

You can't even get to the solitary process of writing a book unless you know and work with many kind, intuitive, and patient people.

"Agent" is not an accurate description for Elias Altman. Yes, he's an agent, he's also an editor, a clear-eyed strategist and calmer of nerves who knows when to hold the line. This book would not have happened without him, and I value his insight and friendship.

Colin Harrison edited this book and gave it shape. I trust our relationship enough, which means when he calls something I wrote "sub-grammatical" I know he's right. Working with the good people at Scribner has been an immense pleasure. Thank you to Brian Belfiglio, Zoey Cole, Sarah Goldberg, and Mark LaFlaur.

John Gall, who designed the book cover, and who's collaborated with me on all my books, and looks at the world in a wonderful and creative way. Derek Brahney, whose drawings help set the tone for each chapter and who's a fellow devotee of New York's un-monuments.

My many angling friends, including Markley Boyer, Joel Stoehr, Matt Hranek, Taite Pearson, Tom Rosenbauer, Matt

ACKNOWLEDGMENTS

McCalla, Verlon Herndon, Michael Williams, and Randy Goldberg, for our time together on and off the water.

My parents, David and Wendy, and my sister, Sarah, angling agnostics all, but who share a love of storytelling, of the pleasures of the table, and a sense of occasion, that I tried to celebrate here.

Finally, and most importantly, to Emilie Hawtin. My partner in all things and a lover of the natural world, who keeps our life together elegantly in balance. Your first trout was a bigger thrill than any I've ever caught.

ABOUT THE AUTHOR

David Coggins is the author of *Men and Manners* and the *New York Times* bestseller *Men and Style*. He writes about fly fishing for *Robb Report* and tailoring, drinking, and travel for numerous publications, including the *Financial Times*, *Bloomberg Pursuits*, and *Condé Nast Traveler*. Coggins lives in New York and fishes regularly in the Catskills, Wisconsin, and Montana.

CPSIA information can be obtained
at www.ICGtesting.com
Printed in the USA
BVHW052342190622
639739BV00003B/2